The SHEFFIELD Cook Book

A celebration of the amazing food & drink on our doorstep
Featuring 50 stunning recipes

The FOREWORD

By Dr G. David Baldwin, Alias 'The Big Un'

What a great idea – an all encompassing Sheffield Cook Book celebrating the best that our region has to offer.

I started in the Sheffield food scene on December 22nd 1954 and apart from my spell in the Merchant Navy and selling pots for the famous Sheffielder 'Potty Edwards', I've been around it ever since.

The food scene has changed so much since I started in 1954/55, when there were very few restaurants of note, of which Tuckwood's was without doubt the field leader. We had Davy's Cafés in the city centre, Thorpe's Café & Restaurant and of course most of what remained of the big stores, Walsh's and Atkinsons (who owned Tuckwood's) – and who could forget Hopkinson's Fish & Chip Emporiums?

Surprisingly, none of the big chains returned to the city after the war and indeed it's true to say that Sheffield became a gastronomic desert until the advent of new generations of food heroes.

How different it is now – with the city centre being overrun by big chain operators who seem to come and go with the wind.

However, despite difficult times recently the entrepreneurial spirit of the gladiators of our food industry has prevailed.

We have a strong field of runners in all sections of the industry who benefit from the strong support of Eat Sheffield and all our friends at Sheffield Hallam University.

Things began to change for the better in the 1950's when a diverse range of cultures began to find fertile ground for their home cuisines. These were almost entirely family businesses; I'm pleased to say that many of them still exist today including Zing Vaa, Ashoka (formerly Shujon – Kamal Ahmed, now in the safe hands of Rahul Amin) and many others.

Around this time Frank & Aldo Bernie brought three of their restaurants to Sheffield; the first chain to return after the war. I always think of them as the patron saints of the industry, without whom most of our mother's and father's generation would never have eaten out in restaurants. The Bernie Inn at Norton became their flagship.

Thank you for buying this book and may I wish you all Bon Appétit!

The CONTENTS

The food

Sheffielders recipes

THANK You

to the following people for making this book possible:

Niki Baker – Eat Sheffield

David Baldwin – Baldwin's Omega

Lee Bullen – Sheffield Wednesday FC

Shaun Doane – Everly Pregnant Brothers

Lesley Draper – Sheffield Telegraph

Jane Fairclough

Andy Gabbitas – The Wortley Arms

Lindsay Garfitt – Seven Hills W.I.

James Hargreaves

Jennifer Marsden – Seven Hills W.I.

Chris Morgan – Sheffield United FC

Janine Morrall

Luke Prest

Rony Robinson – BBC Radio Sheffield

Kim Whelan – Seven Hills W.I.

Written by: Adelle Draper, Carl Reid

Edited by: Phil Turner, Carl Reid

Photography by: Marc Barker, Paul Cocker

Designed by: Paul Cocker

Cover art: Luke Prest, www.lukeprest.com

Additional photography: Polly Baldwin,
Trupix Photography, S6 Photography,
Sheffield Hallam University, Sheffield Telegraph,
Symbios Design

Contributors: Niki Baker, Donna Barker,
Samantha Cocker, Claudia Cole, James Eardley,
Andy Gabbitas, Max Goldbart, Nick Hallam,
Rachel Heward, Jason Keens, Lewis Mottram,
Sarah Wade

Published by Meze Publishing
Blind Mice Media Ltd
Unit 1 Beehive Works
Milton Street
Sheffield S3 7WL
www.mezepublishing.co.uk
Tel: 0114 275 7709

My love affair with food started early. My sister, Karen, and I enjoying a birthday picnic in 1976.

Family meals were a chance for the whole family to spend time together. My sister, Claire, and I were particularly close.

You may think that growing up in Sheffield in the 1970s was a food nightmare; but my early food memories are ones I will cherish.

Dining out was an exotic affair to a child; visits to The Bernie Inn at Norton, and The Sicey at Sheffield Lane Top made me feel grown-up – even if I did then order chicken in a basket and chips (a nightclub staple at the time.)

Street food invariably involved a visit to see my brother, Vincent, who worked at The Wimpy on Fargate to try and cadge a free burger, or standing in Pond Street after daring the top splash at Sheaf Valley Baths with the aroma of fish & chips from the Minerva Café enticing us in. Also let's not forget Greasy Vera's...

Like a lot of families at that time we grew food in the back garden of our council house. Dad grew everything – from the usual suspects of potatoes, tomatoes and carrots to the more exotic offerings of marrows, courgettes and even an attempt at sweetcorn.

I can still remember the taste of a cooked buttery Jersey Royal straight from the garden – I've never tasted one as good since, and probably never will. We had a great deal of success with the marrows; but then ended up throwing them away as my mum didn't know how to cook one.

One fond memory was venturing to see Sheffield Wednesday, though my favourite part was walking past Bassetts to get a sugary whiff of all their delights, because the football was invariably poor.

But I'll never forget the summer of '76 – my birthday party in the garden was the start of my love affair with potted meat and crisp sandwiches (a rare treat for me even today.)

And finally, as an example as to how things have changed; Provenance (sp.) was a place in France when I was growing up.

Paul Cocker

Roast dinners. Apple puff and custard. Macaroni cheese. My mum was no Gordon Ramsay – but like all kids – I loved her cooking. It's only in the last 10 years or so – as I've become reasonably adept in the kitchen myself – that I've realised heating up a few pizzas and oven chips and emptying a can of beans into a saucepan wasn't the most challenging of culinary tasks.

But then again, as so many of us are, my mum was always too busy. Rushing here, there and everywhere, it was a wonder she found time to get tea on the table some nights.

That's one of the reasons why, in recent years, eating out has become such an improved experience – not just here in Sheffield, but across the country. We're all so hectic that sometimes we don't have the energy to cook. So why not eat out?

And, although we may not officially have any Michelin-starred restaurants in the Steel City (though Fischers at Baslow and The Old Vicarage in Ridgeway are so close we may as well claim them as our own), there's no shortage of high quality culinary hotspots.

Establishments such as The Wortley Arms, The Florentine, The Milestone and Nonnas would thrive anywhere – and that's just naming a handful. Which brings us nicely to The Sheffield Cook Book. For those days when you're in the mood to put some effort into your cooking, we've 50 recipes – all created here in Sheffield for you to try. From Ashoka's cricket pakoras to Fancie's corned beef hash with duck egg, there's plenty of ways for you to sample the best that Sheffield has to offer in the comfort of your own home. And, of course, no Sheffield cook book would be complete without a contribution from Henderson's Relish.

So remember, support your locals and, most importantly – get cooking!

Phil Turner

The SHEFFIELD food scene

Sheffield is synonymous with many things. Steel, snooker, real ale … The Full Monty.

Yet there's one thing that all Sheffielders know, but given our dogged Northern nature, very rarely shout about – our glorious city is blessed, truly blessed, with a burgeoning independent food scene.

From bakeries to bistros, markets to Michelin stars, Sheffield offers up the full field to fork experience.

There's a reason why we're often referred to as the biggest village in the world. Aside from the fact you can barely walk 100 yards without bumping into someone you know, the residents here share a fierce passion for their home that you simply won't find in most other cities – working together for the common good and benefit of the community.

Local restaurants use local suppliers wherever and whenever possible – and Sheffield diners will eat independently in a similar vein. It's this 'circle of life' and drive to help each other that makes Sheffield unique – and it's why this book now exists.

Not only will you learn about the specific, wonderful people who give their heart and soul to the Sheffield food scene, you'll also be supporting what they do – enabling them to continue building our city's growing gastronomic reputation.

Hopefully, this will inspire you to think in new ways about shopping, eating and cooking in Sheffield.

So, read on, and enjoy the very best that the Steel City has to offer – tha' knows it makes sense.

Rupert Rowley of Fischers demonstrates a dish at the Sheffield Food Festival. © Sheffield Hallam University

Sheffield Town Hall Square attracts crowds of avid 'foodies' during the Sheffield Food Festival. © Sheffield Hallam University

Eat SHEFFIELD

The Sheffield Cook Book wouldn't have been possible without Eat Sheffield – so just who are this food barmy bunch?

Eat Sheffield is an initiative set up by Sheffield Business School at Sheffield Hallam University, to celebrate and champion the very best independent food places and producers that the city has to offer.

Actively representing and promoting the region's thriving food industry the initiative has evolved into an all-encompassing database of independent food businesses – from restaurants to cafes, butchers to bakers, market traders to community food projects and more – offering a collation of information that's simply vital to the Sheffield food scene.

The whole project is backed by Sheffield Business School – with all services provided free of charge.

It's a scheme that's unique to Sheffield – and one which Sheffield has taken to its heart. Their annual awards have a reputation for credibility, are recognised across the region and have led to winners achieving even higher accolades on a national level.

With thousands of social media followers, they offer an unprecedented platform to local businesses – and the Eat Sheffield badge has now become both a local stamp of approval as well as a symbol of quality and respect.

What's more, the lovely people behind the initiative have been involved within the food industry at all levels. They know what it takes to build a business and to make it a success – and they're passionate about passing this knowledge on to all involved.

Head to www.eatsheffield.com for more.

eat Sheffield

Awards 2013

Sheffield Hallam University | Sheffield Business School

The annual Eat Sheffield Awards have become one of the highlights of the Sheffield food calendar. © Sheffield Hallam University

The SHEFFIELD business school

The food industry can be a tough nut to crack. So, if you're thinking about a pursuing a career within it, you need to surround yourself with the very best in the business.

You'll be pleased to know that the work Eat Sheffield has undertaken with local businesses has helped place the hospitality and food degrees offered within the Service Sector Management department at the heart of the local food scene.

Based within the Sheffield Business School, at Sheffield Hallam University, both the Eat Sheffield and Sheffield Food Festival initiatives have helped SHU in becoming a 'University of Choice' for food based curriculum students – contributing hugely towards the university's 'employability' mission by providing real world opportunities for its students.

The Centre for Food and Hospitality Innovation (with an investment of over £3.5m) is commited to real world learning at a time when many other Universities have chosen to no longer support this crucial aspect of education.

Hospitality students in the first and second year of their course use the facilities to deliver a range of food and beverage experiences; in the final year the culinary arts students further develop this expertise in culinary innovation. The results of this strategy can be seen in their award winning students.

As well as state of the art kitchen facilities, the Food and Nutrition students have the benefit of utilising a wide range of fully equipped, newly refurbished laboratories. These facilities allow students to work alongside industry professionals – helping to solve real life industrial challenges. This not only improves the students' practical skills but enhances future employability opportunities along with placement opportunities.

When it comes to learning about food, this is the place to be. With decades of experience of delivering tourism, hospitality, events and food and nutrition courses, Sheffield Hallam University's staff are in high demand for their industry expertise – offering a cutting edge learning experience. Seriously, what these guys don't know isn't worth knowing (it's no wonder that hospitality and food courses at SHU are consistently ranked in the top five nationally).

Over the years, they've forged extensive links with businesses and organisations both locally, nationally and internationally, and ensure that their courses fully prepare students for a career in the industry.

And, with local honorary doctorates including Sheffield food royalty such as Max Fischer and David Baldwin on board, you know you're in good hands.

See www.shu.ac.uk/sbs for more.

Specialist kitchen facilities within the Centre
for Food & Hospitality Innovation, at SHU

The *SHEFFIELD* food festival

The Sheffield Food Festival has become something of a city institution. Now a staple on the local calendar, the event attracts hundreds of thousands of visitors over three days – making it one of the leading free city centre festivals in the South Yorkshire region.

The urban event is divided into festival areas and acts as a showcase for our regional produce and businesses – celebrating South Yorkshire as a vibrant and diverse culinary destination. It also serves to show, year upon year, exactly how bonkers Sheffield is about food.

Devised, organised and delivered by the Sheffield Food Festival Partnership, (led by Sheffield Business School), the city wide foodathon turns Sheffield into a culinary playground – with a host of demos, masterclasses, special guest appearances, stalls, pop up restaurants and more. As Project Manager, Niki Baker puts it: "It's simply a joy to see places across the city full of people enjoying food. The Sheffield Food Festival is something we're all incredibly proud of."

Supporting the local food economy, the Sheffield Food Festival offers an amazing chance for visitors to sample the local and seasonal delights our region has to offer. It's also an opportunity to learn about different ways of growing and cooking food – plus it provides a fantastic platform to local businesses. As important as it is fun and informative, long may it reign.

Find out more at www.sheffieldfoodfestival.org.

Local radio celebrities Toby Foster and Paulette Edwards compare at the Sheffield Food Festival. © Sheffield Hallam University

GREEN OLIVES
STUFFED ALMONDS

BLACK OLIVES

Morocco or The Moor? – You wouldn't know the difference with the astounding array of olives on display. © Sheffield Hallam University

Shaun Doane & Janine Morrall
MEAT & POTATO PIE WITH HENDO'S

Sheffielders are famed the world over for their friendliness – and you'll not meet a friendlier couple than Shaun Doane and Janine Morrall. Sheffield's answer to 'Posh n' Becks' are well known throughout the city for Shaun's appearances in popular ukele band The Everly Pregnant Brothers, and Janine's hard work with British Cycling's Breeze – an initiative to get women into cycling. You'll often find them at Missie Cindz Pudding Club or supporting many of the great independent cafés, bars and producers that grace this proud city. Serves 4 big 'uns or 6 little 'uns.

Ingredients

For the pastry:

225g plain flour

115g butter (or lard)

Pinch of salt

Pinch of black pepper

Enough cold water to form the dough

For the filling:

1kg potatoes, diced to about 3cm chunks

400g braising steak or stewing beef

1 teaspoon onion salt

1 teaspoon celery salt

2 beef stock cubes

600ml water

Method

To make the pastry:

Blend the flour and butter in a food processor, until it becomes crumb-like and add the water slowly until the dough forms. Knead the dough for 5 minutes then wrap in cling film. Refrigerate for at least 1 hour.

For the filling:

In a saucepan, place the beef, onion salt, celery salt and stock cubes, add the water, bring to the boil and simmer until the meat becomes tender. Boil the diced potatoes for 20 minutes until softened in salted water.

Pre-heat the oven to 200ºc.

Place the meat and half the gravy in the bottom of an ovenproof pie dish, then add a layer of potatoes, roll out the pastry and cover the dish. Bake in the centre of the oven for approximately 30 minutes or until the pastry is golden brown and the filling is bubbling.

Reduce the remaining gravy to thicken and serve the pie with mushy peas, gravy and a good splash or three of Henderson's Relish.

Goes very well with a pint of Thornbridge Sequoia, Kelham Island Best or Bradfield Brown Cow ale!

Bet you look good on the
TANDOOR

Ashoka brought the first Indian restaurant to Sheffield. Nearly half a century later, they still offer authentic, quality Indian food in a relaxed atmosphere.

The exotic aroma of India embraces you from the moment you step into Ashoka. It's distinctive and special – thanks, not just to the spices used, but also to the traditional, charcoal-fuelled, tandoor oven.

Ashoka, named after the great Indian emperor, is a Sheffield institution; a cornerstone of Ecclesall Road since it was opened by Bangladeshi Kamal Ahmed nearly 50 years ago.

Kamal had conducted research by drinking tea in famous restaurants, including London's Dorchester and Savoy hotels, to learn service from the best before heading north. He convinced a local lawyer to invest in his dream – and Ashoka was born in 1967. Kamal worked there until his retirement in 2004 when current owner Rahul Amin took over.

With the business came loyal staff. Kadir Ali has been head chef for over 40 years; tandoori chef Noor Alam has been supporting him for over 2 decades; and some front-of-house staff have racked up over 15 years. Even local suppliers remain loyal (the same local butcher has supplied the restaurant for over 20 years!)

Ashoka attributes its success to authenticity, quality and devoted customers – some of whom have been dining there for decades. It's a social hub where friendships, business partnerships and even relationships have been formed. They're also famed for their creative and imaginative advertisement campaigns. Oh, and it's the Arctic Monkeys' favourite place for a curry.

Grandma's
CRICKET PAKORAS

These pakoras were made by Rahul's grandmother in India whenever the national team played cricket. The family used to gather around the old wireless, eat pakoras and cheer India to a cricketing win. Grandma is no longer with the family but now Dad makes these pakoras as a good luck superstition whenever India is playing!
Makes approximately 20 pakoras.

Ingredients

1 normal tea mug of gram or chickpea flour

Water

1 level teaspoon salt

¼ teaspoon baking powder

½ teaspoon sugar

1 green chilli, chopped

1 medium onion white or red, finely diced

½ medium sized courgette, finely diced

Sunflower or vegetable oil for frying

Method

Sieve the flour into a large bowl. Add salt and baking powder then a little water at a time until you have a thick batter.

Finely dice the onion and courgette and combine with the batter.

Heat the oil to frying temperature (Grandma used to put a little batter into the oil and if the batter rose to the surface within a few seconds it was hot enough).

Using your hand scoop a golf ball sized amount of mixture and place gently into the oil.

Fry until golden (a few minutes).

Serve with Sriracha hot sauce and natural yoghurt or Heinz tomato ketchup (India's favourite condiment) and lime wedges.

*Sriracha hot sauce is made from sun ripened chillies which are ground into a smooth paste along with garlic. It's named after the coastal city of Si Racha.

The beauty and THE BEEF

Baldwin's Omega has an almost legendary reputation in culinary circles; built on impeccable service, flawless presentation and some cracking local beef.

Baldwin's Omega is synonymous with Sheffield food – you can't have one without the other.

Run for over 30 years by Master Chef of Great Britain David Baldwin and his wife Pauline, Baldwin's has developed a reputation as one of the best banqueting venues in the north. This is thanks too to head chef Stephen Roebuck, who's been with the Baldwin's for 25 years.

David, who was born and raised in the Broomhall area of Sheffield, had a passion for food from the time he started his first job at Tuckwood's Restaurant on Surrey Street.

He went on to run the Hillsborough Suite at Sheffield Wednesday's ground, where his oven-to-table banqueting first became famous, and eventually bought the current Baldwin's premises in 1981 – after having worked there as a grill chef in the '60s.

He achieved success through outstanding service, modern British food, and a commitment to using fresh, local produce – especially beef. The lunchtime restaurant is named the Rib Room. Each morning, a full sirloin is cooked and available served three ways – which is something Baldwin's has become known for.

Known affectionately as 'The Big 'Un', David is endearingly renowned for his straight-talking: "A lady once called me over to complain that she'd found a piece of shot in her pheasant. I told her – well it didn't die of a heart attack!"

He has been chairman and president of the National Restaurant Association and was recently awarded an honorary doctorate by Sheffield Hallam University in recognition of his help developing young chefs, commitment to high standards and for his charitable work.

David is often asked the secret behind his success. His response? "There's nothing mysterious about hard work."

Pan-fried sea trout with
KING PRAWNS & WHITE WINE FISH SAUCE

A true classic. Serves 4

Ingredients

4 x 140g tranches of sea trout

1 large glass white wine

2 shallots, finely chopped

100g baby leaf spinach

1 large bulb fennel

½ pint fish stock

55ml double cream

8 king prawns

2 tomatoes

Watercress

Method

Pre-heat the oven to 160°c.

Peel the bulb of fennel and slice lengthways into quarters.

Place in an oven proof dish with garlic and a splash of olive oil. Cover with water, place foil over the top and bake for 1 hour.

Bring the fish stock to the boil, add the white wine and reduce by half.

Heat a frying pan, add the shallots and cook – make sure they don't colour.

Add the reduced fish stock and cream to the shallots and leave to simmer.

Skin, de-seed and chop the tomatoes and leave to one side.

In another large frying pan, place the sea trout skin side down until the skin starts to crisp. Turn and place in a hot oven at 180°c for 5 minutes.

Meanwhile, fry the spinach in a separate pan and keep warm.

Add the prawns to the sea trout and return to the oven for a further 8 minutes.

Place the spinach in a dish then add the sea trout, prawns and seasoned sauce to serve.

Sprinkle with diced tomato and top with micro herbs.

Walkin' on the BEECHES

From butcher's assistant to one of the best delicatessens in the North –
Chris & Donna Beech are at the forefront of Sheffield's food revolution.

The story of Beeches of Walkley is one of natural evolution.

After 15 years at the South Road shop's butcher's counter working as an assistant, Chris Beech took over in 2010.

He continued to run the small counter at one end of a large convenience store with wife Donna – and developed the offering by sourcing local meats, free range produce and more unusual cuts.

With custom and demand for fresh, local produce building, the Beeches recognised an opportunity to expand and took on an empty unit across the road. They transformed it into a greengrocers and welcomed the challenge of learning a new trade while further supporting the community and keeping trade local.

Shortly after, competition from a nearby chain supermarket signalled the end of the convenience store adjacent to the butchers shop and, once again, opportunity knocked.

Section by section, the Beeches took over the old store, first incorporating a rainbow hued greengrocery and closing down the separate shop. A deli, frozen foods and a wealth of local produce followed – and was so popular that their first Christmas saw queues around the block.

Brands such as The Sheffield Honey Company, Whirlow Hall Farm, nearby breweries and their own labelled items take pride of place alongside the Sheffield Secret Sausage –

a best-seller using a well-known ingredient made in the city for over 100 years.

Beeches has succeeded in revitalising Walkley's shopping experience and boasts a strong community focus – listening to customers' requests and delivering to locals come sun or snow. It's brought the farm shop ethos to the inner city.

Beeches tribute to
T'OLE IN T' ROAD

A large traditional Yorkshire pudding, Beeches' award-winning Sheffield Secret Sausages, gravy and vegetables. Serves 4

Ingredients

For the Yorkshire Pudding:

4 heaped tablespoons plain flour

½ teaspoon salt

3 medium free range eggs from Whirlow Hall Farm

275ml full fat milk from Our Cow Molly

2 teaspoons vegetable or sunflower oil plus extra for greasing

For the gravy:

1 jar Beeches beef stock

1 tablespoon sea salt

1 onion, finely chopped

225ml Beeches Brew by Bradfield Brewery

2 teaspoons plain flour

2 teaspoons water

8 Sheffield Secret Sausages

Roasted veg:

Choose any vegetables you like. We opted for; carrots, parsnips, red onion, shallots, courgettes, mixed peppers, mushrooms, swede, potatoes

Rapeseed oil

Rosemary

Thyme

Paprika

Black pepper

For the mashed potatoes:

1-2 medium white potatoes per person

Butter and cream from Longley Farm

Method

For the Yorkshire Pudding:

Sift the flour and salt into a bowl.

Gradually whisk in the beaten eggs and milk until the batter has the consistency of single cream. Set aside to rest for an hour.

Add in chopped onion then drizzle oil into a pudding tray and heat until smoking hot. Quickly fill with the batter using a ladle.

Bake at 220°c for 25-30 minutes or until pudding is risen and golden brown.

For the vegetables:

Pre-heat the oven to 190°c.

Prepare the vegetables of your choice and cut them into chunks. Bring to the boil in water then drain.

Place the rapeseed oil in an oven proof dish and roast the vegetables for 45 minutes.

For the potatoes:

Peel and chop the potatoes, place in a saucepan and cover with water. Bring to the boil and add salt to taste.

Simmer for 20 minutes then mash and add a large knob of butter and two tablespoons of cream.

For the gravy and sausages:

Fry the onions in oil until softened. Add beef stock and ale, then bring to the boil. Reduce the heat and simmer for 10 minutes. Sausages can be fried, grilled or oven baked.

Singin' the BLOO'S

Bloo88 has a prestigious history in the make-up of our fair city – the site of the famed Hallamshire Hotel is taking the legacy of this great pub to new levels.

The name Bloo 88 is undoubtedly one that sticks in the mind... but just where it came from, nobody can quite remember.

Some say it stems from Chinese lucky numbers, others that it was just a catchy nonentity. But one thing's certain: Bloo 88's recipe of pizzas, cocktails and 'love' is one of success.

Located on the site of the former Hallamshire Hotel in West Street, Bloo 88 has become well known for its stone-baked pizzas. The restaurant and bar's focal feature is a roaring open pizza oven; its flickering flames adding to the industrial ambiance of the cavernous interior which is full of stripped red brick and reclaimed furniture.

It's a social space that makes people feel comfortable and welcome – but the team like to put a spin on classics when it comes to food and drink. Pizzas are made fresh by hand every day and the menu includes specialities like the Kingston

Five, with Reggae Reggae sauce and jerk chicken, and the Spanish-influenced El Mariachi – with lashings of salsa and sour cream.

The cocktail list, which features around 20 concoctions, includes a lychee martini, the exotic Bloo Passion (using Malibu and pineapple) and a special created using local brand O'Hara's rum – combining a refreshing mix of limes, honey, mint and ginger beer.

Most evenings at Bloo 88 are themed – with regulars turning out for salsa nights, lounge music, funk & soul sessions and pop at the weekend.

The bar and restaurant offers something for everyone and has become one of the city centre's perfect places to socialise, dine and drink whatever the occasion.

The Bloo 88
SHEFFIELD PIZZA & COCKTAIL

Sheffield has inspired many things over the years – football and steel being just two of them – but we think this is the first time it has ever inspired a delicious pizza & cocktail combination.

Ingredients

For the pizza:

350g pizza dough

For the tomato base:

3 tablespoons Henderson's Relish

100ml spiced tomato pizza sauce

100g grated mozzarella cheese

For the topping:

1 parsnip, peeled and sliced

1 carrot, peeled and sliced

1 potato, peeled and sliced

8 cauliflower florets

Handful of garden peas

1 teaspoon jerk seasoning

100g cooked chicken

For the cocktail:

50ml O'Hara's Spiced Rum

1 bottle ginger beer

6 fresh lime slices

Sprig of fresh mint

1 tablespoon The Sheffield Honey Company blossom honey

Handful of crushed ice

Method

For the pizza:

Peel and slice the parsnip and carrots into 2cm thick slices.

In boiling salted water, parboil the cauliflower, carrots, parsnips, potato and garden peas.

Cut the parboiled potato into thin slices

Marinate the chicken in Henderson's Relish and jerk seasoning.

Mix a ladleful of the pizza sauce with 3 teaspoons of Henderson's Relish.

Pull out the pizza dough to form a thin base then top the pizza base with the sauce.

Spread the thin slices of potato over the sauce then cover with a handful of mozzarella cheese.

Spread the carrots, parsnips, cauliflower, garden peas and marinated chicken over the pizza.

Drizzle on some more Henderson's Relish.

To cook:

If you're lucky enough to have a stone pizza oven then paddle into the oven for 5-6 minutes at 280-320˚c. Alternatively cook in the oven on a pizza tray or stone for around 15-20 minutes at 220˚c.

Leave to cool, add another drizzle of Hendersons Relish, slice and enjoy!

For the cocktail:

Muddle the fresh limes and honey in the bottom of your glass, add a handful of fresh mint, then top up the glass with crushed ice.

Pour O'Hara's Spiced Rum over the ice.

Stir with the flat end of a bar spoon then top up with ginger beer.

Garnish with a topping of crushed ice, a sprig of mint and some drizzled honey.

Lee Bullen's
YORKSHIRE FISHCAKE

In Yorkshire, we know that a fishcake should be two slices of potato
sandwiching beautiful white fish – the rest of the country is just plain wrong.
So, who to ask to cook one of Sheffield's finest dishes?
A Scotsman, obviously – after all, it is deep fried.
Lee Bullen is a hero to the blue and white contingent of the city –
who captained Sheffield Wednesday to promotion in front of 40,000+ fans
at The Millennium Stadium, Cardiff.
Bully's been around – playing professional football in Scotland, Hong Kong,
Australia, Greece and England – and his versatility has seen him take to the
field in all eleven positions for The Owls.
We hooked him up with master chef Andy Gabbitas
at The Wortley Arms to showcase his culinary talents.

Ingredients

For the beer batter:

150g self-raising flour

Large pinch of salt & pepper

220ml Wentworth Best Bitter or
your favourite local ale

For the fish cakes:

16 slices potatoes, each 5mm thick

450g fish fillets, (cod or haddock)

1 dash of plain flour, for dusting

Method

To make the batter:

Put the flour, salt and pepper in a bowl. Make a well in the centre and pour in ¾ of the
beer, combine then keep adding small amounts until it's the consistency of double cream.
Leave to stand.

Peel and parboil two large baking potatoes, such as King Edwards. Allow to cool then cut
into 5mm thick slices.

Sandwich the pieces of fish between two pieces of potato. Dip the cakes into flour and
shake off the excess, then dip into the batter to cover well. Shake off any excess.

Season with salt and pepper.

Heat the oil in a deep fat fryer to 190°c. Carefully drop a fish cake into the hot fat and let
it settle to the bottom. Add another couple of fish cakes if there's room. They will rise to
the top when hot enough; this should take about 5 minutes.

Turn them over, then leave to cook for another 5 minutes until brown. Remove from the
fryer and drain well on kitchen paper.

Serve with minted mushy peas, tartar sauce and a wedge of lemon.

Ethical COFFEE

Sheffield coffee company Cafeology do things the right way – so you can be assured that your morning 'cup of joe' is fair and ethical.

Most of us don't consider the origins of our morning cup of coffee, but Cafeology's founder, Bryan Unkles, knows the process from start to finish – and takes a hands-on approach to the business.

Having spent years working for other coffee companies, Bryan developed a passion to create his own brand that would import and sell coffee in the most ethical ways possible. And so in 2004 Cafeology was born.

Quality and ethics have always been at the forefront of the business: the company uses only speciality grade Arabica coffees and buys directly from growers in Colombia, El Salvador, Guatemala and Costa Rica before importing straight into the UK.

This commitment has enabled Bryan to forge long-standing relationships with producers, such as Colombian coffee grower Francisco Herrera.

Bryan first flew out to meet Francisco and his team, who are based in Apia in Risaralda, Colombia, in 2009. Since then, Francisco has made a return trip to the UK, to better understand their combined business and see the fruits of his labour being enjoyed in Sheffield.

Cafeology's strong focus on quality has resulted in a range of products carrying recognised marks such as Fairtrade, Soil Association and Rainforest Alliance, ensuring a fair deal for the farmers whose crops they buy, while also making Cafeology's products fully traceable.

Their good work extends further still through their relationship with Coffee Kids, an organisation working with coffee-farming communities throughout Latin America to create projects in such areas as education, healthcare and economic diversification.

Demand for Cafeology products has also led to expansion into tea, hot chocolate and cold drinks under the Teaology, Cocoaology and Frappeology brands, as well as the founding of boutique coffee brand Café Cereza.

And it's not just Sheffield that has fallen in love with the tasty beverages. The company operates on a national scale, working with a range of universities, businesses and independent outlets. But they are extremely proud of their Sheffield heritage – they work with local charities and are strident supporters of Eat Sheffield, whose Favourite Café award they have sponsored for the past few years.

To enjoy the benefits of Cafeology's exacting ethical standards, look out for their drinks at outlets in and around Sheffield – or visit the company's first coffee pod, open daily at Decathlon near the bottom of The Moor.

From the cherry
TO THE CUP

The journey of your Cafeology coffee from Latin America

Francisco's cooperative lies within the stunning Tatama National Park where all the coffee is picked by hand at altitude around 1400 meters.

Workers for the cooperative are paid a fair daily wage, rather than money per kilo picked, which enables them to spend time in the fields hand selecting the best coffee cherries from each plant.

When the cherries are ripe for picking they are processed using the wet process method giving a cleaner, more acidic coffee with a fresh finish.

Once through the various stages of soaking and pulping, the parchment beans are rinsed, drained and spread out to dry naturally in the sun on both large patios and wire mesh platforms.

The beans are then shipped to the UK where Cafeology roasts them to their own special recipe. Finally, they are packaged and delivered to restaurants, cafés and other businesses ready to be made into the perfect cup of coffee, however you like it.

Cafeology continue to be at the forefront of ethical sourcing which has seen the introduction of the world's first certified Carbon Neutral coffee from Coope Dota in Costa Rica as well as the launch of the very first RSPB endorsed coffee from Guatemala under the Smithsonian Institution certification.

From farm TO FORK

The Casa Hotel is seriously impressive and offers some of the finest accommodation in our region – but it's the restaurant and their produce that's getting us excited...

When Steve Perez set out to build Chesterfield's four-star Casa Hotel, he wanted its restaurant to be one he'd want to dine in himself – one that could stand alone without the accommodation.

Steve had always been around the hospitality industry. His Barcelonan father, Santiago Garcia Perez, ran Chesterfield's well-known Red Lion pub at Stanage while Steve was growing up – which led to Steve training there as a chef after leaving school.

After spending a few years chasing the wet-led side of the business, and founding the multi-million pound Global Brands drinks company, Steve was keen to follow his other passion – food – as well as to build something special for his home town.

November 2010 saw the opening of the £20million Casa, (meaning 'house') – Chesterfield's only four star hotel.

Its Cocina restaurant reflects Steve's heritage – serving contemporary British food with a Spanish influence. It's simple food, perfectly executed using fresh, quality ingredients, which is evident in the Cocina's two AA rosette rating.

Most notable is the fact that most of Casa's meat comes from its own organic farm, Walton Lodge, just four miles down the road.

Breeds include Belted Galloway cattle, British Saddleback pigs and Grey Faced Dartmoor sheep. All the meat is butchered locally and allowed to mature to tenderise and intensify its natural flavour.

Casa has become a much-loved part of Chesterfield's skyline. It's run by locals, and caters for them too, alongside the multitude of tourists and business people passing through.

Steve's Casa is your casa.

Chilli & lavender scented
WALTON LODGE PORK BELLY

Ingredients

For the dry rub:
226g pork belly per person
50g Maldon salt
Zest of 1 orange
2 cloves garlic, chopped
20g rosemary, chopped
20g thyme, chopped
20g dried lavender
20g dried chilli

For the pork belly:
2 cloves garlic, chopped
20g rosemary, chopped
20g thyme, chopped
20g dried lavender
20g dried chilli
500g goose fat
1 litre vegetable oil

For the sauerkraut:
½ red cabbage, finely shredded
½ spring cabbage, finely shredded
2 carrots, grated
2 shallots, finely sliced
2 cloves garlic, crushed
20g thyme, chopped
Juice of ½ lemon
50g sugar
100ml cider vinegar

For the fondant potato:
6 medium sized Maris Piper potatoes
Enough of the strained goose fat to cover the potatoes
1 bay leaf
6 peppercorns
1 clove garlic
4 sprigs thyme
Maldon salt
50g butter

For the chilli and lavender glaze:
75ml honey
10g lavender seeds
1 red chilli, deseeded and finely chopped

For the red wine and apple sauce:
500ml red wine
50ml Port
50ml Madeira
2 pints fresh beef stock
4 large shallots, chopped
1 carrot, chopped
2 sticks celery, chopped
3 peppercorns
1 bay leaf
3 sprigs thyme
50g cold butter, diced
1 Granny Smith apple, peeled and finely diced
50 chives, finely chopped

Method

For the dry rub:

Combine the ingredients in a bowl, massage into the pork belly and leave on a lipped tray at room temperature for 3 hours.

For the pork belly:

Wash the dry rub off the pork in cold water and dry well with kitchen paper. Heat the oil and goose fat with the other ingredients in a deep sided baking tray – don't get the oil too hot or the garlic will colour and make the oil bitter.

When the goose fat has melted, lower the pork in, cover with foil and place in a pre-heated oven at 140°c for 2½-3 hours.

When tender leave the pork to cool in the oil until it is at a safe temperature to handle.

Remove from the fat and place on a greaseproof lined lipped baking sheet with another sheet on top of the pork. Put a flat tray on the top of this and add weight to it. Leave for at least 4 hours or preferably overnight.

Reserve the cooking oil to cook the fondant potatoes in.

For the sauerkraut:

Sweat off the shallots and garlic in a pan then add the cabbage and carrot and cook until al dente. Deglaze the pan with the cider vinegar and reduce the liquid by half. Add the sugar, lemon juice and chopped thyme, bring to a simmer then remove from the heat. Stir in cabbage and season to taste with salt and pepper.

While still hot place in a bowl and cover with cling film. Once cool place in the fridge for at least 24 hours to ferment.

For the fondant potatoes:

Cut the potatoes into rectangles. Fry the potatoes in goose fat on both sides until golden brown. Season well then cover with the remaining fat.

Add the butter and simmer until the potatoes are cooked all the way through.

For the chilli and lavender glaze:

Heat all the ingredients and simmer until the flavours have infused.

For the red wine and apple sauce:

Add a splash of vegetable oil to a heated pan then add the carrot, celery and shallots. When nicely browned add the red wine, bay leaf, thyme and peppercorns and bring to the boil. Reduce the wine until it has nearly evaporated then add the Port and Madeira. Boil for a minute or so to remove the bitter alcohol flavour and then add the beef stock.

Reduce until the sauce is the consistency of single cream. Pass the liquid through a fine sieve. When ready to serve, bring the sauce back to the boil and whisk in the cold butter for a glossy finish. Add the diced apple and chives just before serving.

To serve:

Cut the pork belly into the desired portion sizes.

Pre-heat the oven to 180°c. Place the potatoes on greaseproof paper in the oven for roughly 10 minutes.

Fry the pork belly on all sides until golden brown and then place on the same tray as the potatoes in the oven. Baste with the chilli and lavender glaze and leave until heated through. Warm the sauerkraut on the stove and check the seasoning. We serve the dish with a few pieces of purple sprouting broccoli but French beans would be a good alternative.

Cruz CONTROL

Visiting Cubana is more than a meal – it's a cultural experience. Latin flair and passion pervade from every nook & cranny of this charming and popular Sheffield hotspot.

Salsa beats compete with a buzz of conversation as diners indulge in mojitos and tapas against a backdrop of pastel-washed walls and worn wooden floors.

Stepping into Cubana conjures up images of dusty Havana and the hot Caribbean sun as the shadowy, atmospheric bar, brings Latino spirit to life.

But the atmosphere is where the Cuban influence stops. The menu is full of Spanish and Latin American dishes – cooked by head chef Fabian Cruz who's led the kitchen since day one. The restaurant's popularity since it opened in November 2000 is testament to his abilites.

Tapas favourites include their famous albondigas (fresh beef meatballs), gambas tigres (tiger prawns) and calamares a la Andaluza (light, crispy squid). They line up next to more unusual creations such as croquetas de pescado (white fish croquettes with saffron rice), merluza al horno (hake and Mediterranean vegetables) and cerdo y calabacin (a South American speciality pork casserole).

The restaurant grew out of Viva Salsa, a Latin music and dance night in Sheffield frequented by hundreds in the mid '90s and run by Cubana's owner Adrian Bagnoli. Music is still integral to the eatery's identity – with live acts or dancing showcased every night of the week. Even Cuban music legends, the Buena Vista Social Club have stamped their seal of approval, visiting the restaurant every time they play in Sheffield.

Cubana has the perfect ingredients for a full evening's entertainment under one roof – the authentic combination of music, food, drink and service is unrivalled in the city.

Merluza
SALSA SAMBUCA

Fillet of hake served with fresh tomatoes in a creamy Sambuca sauce. Serves 4

Ingredients

4 hake fillets (1 per person)

500ml single cream

500ml white wine

6 fresh tomatoes, chopped

200ml Sambuca

Large handful of fresh parsley, chopped

Salt & pepper to season

Method

Place the cream and white wine in a pan and simmer gently.

Add in the chopped fresh tomatoes and pinch of salt then cook until the stock is reduced by half.

Add the fresh hake fillets and simmer for 5 minutes. Turn the fillets and simmer for a further 5 minutes.

Just before serving, turn the gas up high, pour the Sambuca over the dish and carefully flambé.

Garnish with fresh parsley and serve.

Mariscos
CON VINO BLANCO

Hake fillet pieces, mussels and prawns cooked with fresh leeks, potatoes, white wine and cream. Serves 4

Ingredients

100g mussel meat

100g peeled prawns

100g hake fillet (or substitute white fish), diced

100g leeks, diced

100g potatoes, parboiled and sliced

1 glass medium white wine

½ pint double cream

Method

Place the leeks in a hot pan with a touch of olive oil and sweat them down for a couple of minutes.

Add the diced hake fillets, mussels, potatoes, white wine and cream then season with salt and pepper and bring to the boil for 1 minute.

Add the peeled prawns, simmer for a further minute and serve.

Garnish with fresh parsley and serve with your choice of accompaniment. We like rice or cous cous – you could even keep it simple with fresh bread or toast!

The Master CUTLER

Putting Sheffield on the curry map has always been the goal of Cutler's Spice head chef Allam. Now his fresh and vibrant dishes are challenging perceptions of Indian food and driving them to new levels.

As a teenager, Allam Shah Ullah had a vision – that he would one day transform the Cutler's Arms pub at Gleadless into a fantastic Indian restaurant.

He spent the next 15 years working in his family's food outlets in Sheffield, Chesterfield and Doncaster, honing his skills both front and back of house. Then, Allam's almost life-long dream became a reality – when the Cutler's Arms came up for auction and his family secured the deal.

Cutler's Spice opened in October 2011 with Allam running front of house and father Noim and his wife Ashfum Nesa Begum sharing the role of head chef.

The family set out to create a brand for Sheffield – an Indian restaurant that would put the city on the curry map and be big enough to compete with the larger Indian chains.

And the result is visually stunning. White leather chairs and black velvet booths are offset by opulent contemporary crystal chandeliers, exotic carvings and wall-length murals.

The food is equally memorable – hence the reason you'll struggle to get a table in the 200-seater restaurant at the weekend. Allam believes it's his mum's experience that sets the restaurant apart. She's the only female Indian chef working in the city and brings a lifetime's experience to the table.

HYATT
TASTE OF BRITAIN
JAGUAR
AIR INDIA
INDRA TRAVEL
NATCO
CurryLife

The award-winning Cutler's Spice prides itself on employing locally and supporting the community. Ingredients and drinks are sourced from local businesses including Parkway Markets, Arif Food and HP Clarke – ensuring that money goes back into the local economy. The kitchen team makes everything fresh on the premises each day and opens over lunchtime in order to prepare.

Not content to settle, and driven by ambition, Allam wanted to develop his own skills in the kitchen. Inspired by fine dining and Michelin-starred chefs, he aspired to follow the lead of Indian chefs in the '80s – inventing dishes and refining presentation.

Noim could teach him to a degree but presentation wasn't his forte, so he advised Allam to enrol in college. Allam is now the only qualified Bangladeshi chef in Sheffield – with an NVQ Level 3 cooking diploma.

While his training was traditionally British, skills like using knives properly and working on presentation have reignited Allam's enthusiasm for creativity. A sprinkling of dishes on the Cutler's Spice menu – such as Chicken Handi, Towa Chicken and Cutler's Special Biryani – are his own creations. The use of whole, toasted spices, sets them apart from the rest of the menu.

Allam's creative flair has also been recognised by the media – especially Curry Life magazine. His involvement with the publication has seen him travel to India, Slovenia and Sweden to take part in a variety of features in their Taste of Britain project.

And while Allam is keen to introduce more of his dishes and some fine dining to the menu, he recognises it wouldn't be in keeping with the rest of the offering – and the dream of another new restaurant for such fare is forming.

"Determination and caring is the key to success," Allam believes. "If you don't push yourself out of your comfort zone, and create a name for yourself, you'll never get anywhere."

Baked lime & chilli
COD WITH GRAPE CHUTNEY

This recipe shows that you don't have to stick to the 'usual suspects' when cooking Indian food. It's a fusion of European and Indian flavours, the latter coming from the grape salsa which Allam ate as a child and is common in Bangladesh.

Ingredients

2 cod fillets

1 whole lime

1 whole dried red chilli, crushed

50g fresh white grapes

1 garlic clove, very finely chopped

Coriander, very finely chopped

½ teaspoon chilli powder

½ teaspoon turmeric powder

½ teaspoon coriander powder

½ teaspoon jeera powder

250ml red wine

2 tablespoons sugar

1 wedge lemon

2 teaspoons mustard oil

Salt

1 green chilli, very finely chopped

Handful of cranberries

Method

For the fish:

Dry the cod fillets with a paper towel. Cut a lime in half and squeeze over the fish. Sprinkle with the crushed dried red chilli and salt then place on a baking tray in the oven for about 15 minutes at around 190°c.

For the grape chutney:

Roughly dice the grapes, add the garlic, coriander and green chilli with a pinch of salt and mix, then place aside.

For the red wine jus:

In a pan, pour in the red wine, sugar, cranberries, turmeric, chilli powder, jeera and coriander powder then bring to the boil. Reduce the sauce until thickened and the cranberries have more or less dissolved.

For the salad dressing:

Mix the mustard oil and lemon juice with the same amount of water then mix well with the salad leaves of your choice.

To serve:

Place the salad on plate then the grape chutney on top. Gently place the baked fish on top of this and drizzle the jus around the fish and chutney.

Let them EAT CAKE

A doyenne of the Sheffield food scene – Fancie has evolved from the popular cupcake emporium, to a 'must visit' dinner destination with class.

While Fancie will always be known for its delicious cupcakes, there's a lot more to the business these days than sugar and spice.

Founded by trained pastry chef Amanda Perry in 2007, Fancie began life as a craft bakery. Amanda's wares were popular, and she opened a cupcake shop and cafe on Sharrow Vale Road in 2009.

The Fancie offering grew, giving customers greater choice as signature milkshakes, 'cake shakes' and luxurious hot chocolates were added to the menu.

Excited by the company's organic development, and keen to evolve further still, Amanda opened a site on Ecclesall Road in December 2012. This new Fancie – a bakery, canteen and events space offered a more sophisticated appeal.

Stripped back brickwork and reclaimed furniture sets the scene – while the food offering has upped the game. The kitchen, run by respected chef John Parsons, serves rustic, farmhouse style meals – food that people want to eat, not what the chef wants to cook.

This 'comfort food' is an eclectic mix of sharing platters, Asian fusion, American dishes and English classics. The drinks list offers a selection of wines, craft beers, ciders, Prosecco and cocktails.

Around 90% of Fancie's produce is sourced locally from suppliers including Our Cow Molly, Moss Valley, J.H. Mann and Howe's, and the kitchen and bakery teams make everything fresh on the premises.

It all means that these days Fancie is the perfect place for breakfast, lunch, dinner – or cupcakes!

RECIPES

Ask us about Fancie by Night

Corned beef
HASH WITH DUCK EGG

Ingredients

1 whole beef shin, de-boned and cured in a brine for 2 days

2 litres water

100g salt

50g sugar

Pinch pink peppercorns

1 carrot, chopped

4 onions

1 stick celery

2 bay leaves

1kg Maris Piper potatoes

Oil

3 tablespoons wholegrain mustard

100g capers, chopped

100g gherkins, chopped

4 tablespoons tomato ketchup

4 tablespoons brown sauce

1 duck egg per person

Salt & pepper

For the caper butter:

175g unsalted butter

4 tablespoons lemon juice

3 tablespoons capers, rinsed

2 tablespoons roughly chopped flatleaf parsley

Method

To make the brine, combine the water, salt, sugar and pink peppercorns in a large pan and cure the whole beef shin in the brine for 2 days.

After 2 days, rinse the meat under running cold water for 10 minutes. Put the meat in a large pan and cover with water.

Add the carrot, celery, one onion and the bay leaves to the meat. Simmer for around 4 hours until the meat is falling apart.

Meanwhile, peel and soak the Maris Piper potatoes.

Slice the remaining onions as thinly as possible and caramelise in a drop of oil in a large pan. Season with a pinch of salt and pepper – when ready the onions should be golden in colour.

Dice the potatoes into rough 2cm cubes and parboil until just tender.

Drain and spread out on a tray and leave to dry out.

Drain off all liquid from the meat and remove the vegetables and bay leaves.

Mix the meat, potatoes and onions with the wholegrain mustard, capers, gherkins, ketchup and brown sauce.

Press into a terrine mould. Chill for at least 6 hours until firm.

For the caper butter:

Place the butter into a small saucepan over a medium heat and heat until melted and just turning nut brown in colour.

Add the lemon juice, capers and parsley and stir through.

To serve:

Slice and pan fry on both sides until golden and serve with a fried duck egg and caper butter.

A modern CLASSIC

Fischer's at Baslow Hall, is one of the jewels in our region's culinary crown. Offering Michelin-starred dining with luxurious accommodation and first class facilities.

Fischer's restaurant has become the pièce de résistance of Baslow Hall, Derbyshire, thanks to foundations built by owners Max and Susan Fischer and the subsequent work of current head chef Rupert Rowley, who joined them 12 years ago.

The restaurant was awarded a Michelin star under Max Fischer in 1994 and has retained the honour ever since – alongside three AA Rosettes, Good Food Guide listings and many more accolades – which Rupert believes is thanks to their constant ambition to exceed expectations.

He and his team cook with the seasons and make use of some of the finest British ingredients available. Over 90% of the produce used is British, with much of it sourced a stone's throw away from suppliers such as Brock & Morton Rapeseed Oil at Ashford-in-the-Water, Pollard's coffee and The Sheffield Honey Company – which has installed Fischer's own bee hives on the grounds. Dishes are served up on hand-thrown stoneware plates made in the village at Baslow Pottery.

The Fischer's kitchen garden is also an abundant source of produce including a wide range of fruit, vegetables and herbs, which are picked daily by the chefs.

As well as their Classic Menu, the Taste of Britain and Weekend Lunch Menu have become popular. The Taste of Britain menu takes diners on a culinary tour of the British Isles, from Yorkshire game to hand-dived scallops and coastal samphire, while the latter treats guests to a luxurious, memorable menu inspired by home-grown seasonal produce sourced from the hall's grounds.

And the setting couldn't be better suited to this award-winning cooking. Built in 1907 from locally-quarried gritstone, Baslow Hall makes an impressive sight as you reach the top of its winding, tree-lined driveway.

The Fischer's, who fell in love with it back in 1988, have lovingly restored the house and gardens to their present glory. As well as the restaurant, the hall boasts six guest bedrooms in the main building and five in the garden house, as well as facilities for business meetings and intimate weddings.

Whatever the time of year, Rupert's creative menus feature superbly executed dishes comprising local, seasonal produce, modern techniques and exquisite presentation.

Yorkshire Blue
AND SHEFFIELD HONEY

Serves 10 as a starter

Ingredients

For the blue cheese mousse:

200g whipping cream

50g milk

150g Yorkshire Blue cheese, crumbled

2g gellan gum type F

Salt to taste

For the honey glaze:

250g water

50g sugar

150g The Sheffield Honey Co. Heather Honey

11g pectin

For the brioche:

660g strong bread flour

5 free range eggs, beaten

20g fresh yeast

30g sugar

15g salt

60g tepid water

250g butter, at room temperature

To garnish:

The Sheffield Honey Co. honeycomb

Salad leaves

Method

For the brioche:

Mix together the flour, salt and sugar in a large bowl.

In another bowl, dissolve the yeast in the water, then whisk in the eggs.

Add the wet mixture to the flour and bring together to form a dough. Knead for 15 minutes before adding the butter in small amounts to the dough. Alternatively, place all the ingredients except the butter in a mixer with a dough hook and knead for 10 minutes, then mix in the butter.

Leave the dough to chill in the fridge for 12 hours or overnight. Weigh into 18g pieces and roll into small buns. Leave somewhere warm to prove until doubled in size. Bake at 200°c for 10-15 minutes until golden brown.

For the blue cheese mousse:

Bring the cream, milk and gellan gum to the boil in a saucepan, whisking continually. Pour over the Yorkshire Blue Cheese and blend together until emulsified. Season with salt to taste and cool in the fridge.

For the honey glaze:

Mix together the sugar and pectin. In a saucepan, add all the ingredients and bring to the boil while whisking. Once boiled, remove from the heat and leave to cool.

To assemble:

Take each brioche bun and cut the top off. With a small knife hollow out the centre until you are just left with a shell. Fill the brioche with the blue cheese mousse then place the top back on the bun.

Brush the honey glaze over the top and sides of the bun. Place in an oven at 200°c for 6 minutes. Remove from the oven and brush with the honey glaze again. Place a small piece of fresh honeycomb on each bun and serve with mixed salad leaves.

New kids on THE BLOCK

Already a landmark, The Florentine (formerly the Fulwood Inn) is making a strong impression on the Sheffield food scene with good local food in a stunning setting.

It may be a relative newcomer to the Sheffield food scene, but The Florentine has already stamped its mark by winning Exposed Magazine's best newcomer.

The interior, which sympathetically melds modern fixtures with the original features of the 1900s private town house, is the handiwork of Sheffield designer Laura Lowe – and, despite being part of a small independent chain, its local influence doesn't stop there.

Head chef and local lad Jon Mahoney has helped develop the restaurant's core menu and created their bestselling beef short rib – slow-cooked overnight in their Josper oven and smothered in sticky barbecue sauce to deliver bold flavours in every mouthful.

His specials are meat-led, with cuts being supplied by Yorkshire butcher John Penny & Son. Stay over in one of The Florentine's 11 boutique-style bedrooms and you'll find complimentary chocolates from Ecclesall Road chocolatiers Cocoa too.

Over 400 pizzas a week fly out of their wood-fired pizza oven, the fuel for which (along with the Josper coal) is also locally sourced.

Manager and Sheffielder, Andy Nulty, has also had heavy input in stocking the bar with a selection of local beers.

With premium casual dining, lots of local influence and an expansive, tiered beer garden that offers the perfect setting for summer al fresco dining, The Florentine offers something for everyone.

Bbq & honey
SMOKED SHORT RIBS

This is one of my favourite rib recipes as it brings out the best in the meat, with little fuss, while enhancing the flavour.

Ingredients

1 full beef short rib, cut down the bone

400g barbecue sauce

125g honey

70g ketchup

35ml soy sauce

300ml beef stock

Method

You ideally need to smoke the ribs outdoors on the bbq. The best way to do this is to put the ribs on just as the flames are dying down, close all vents and cover with the lid.

Smoke for 4-5 minutes, turning frequently – smoke should billow out everywhere, that's fine!

Once smoked, allow to cool slighty and then place the smoked ribs into a deep casserole dish.

Mix together the barbecue sauce, honey, ketchup and soy then pour over the ribs. Add the beef stock until the ribs are just covered

Double wrap the dish in foil and braise at 160°c for around 6 hours.

Once cooked gently remove the short ribs and reduce the remaining sauce in a pan to thicken.

Serve with thick cut chips, a green side salad and your choice of sides, such as coleslaw and potato salad.

Rony Robinson's
SPICY AUBERGINE & TOMATO

Rony Robinson is mischievous. Listen to him on the radio and you'll know this –
be interviewed by him and it's even more apparent.

But, behind the impish glint, lies a rare talent. An author, teacher and playwright,
but he's best known to most Sheffielders as the daily voice on BBC Radio Sheffield's
lunchtime show for the last 30 years.

An alumni of King Ted's & Keble College, Oxford, he also holds an honorary doctorate
from Sheffield Hallam University. He also supports Sheffield United.

This dish was inspired by Rony's huge collection of Madhur Jaffrey cookbooks and
combines a mixture of middle eastern spices to give you a beautifully aromatic curry
without the inclusion of garlic or cooked onions.

Ingredients

For the basmati rice:

200g basmati rice

2 bay leaves

For the aubergines:

2 aubergines

50g plain flour

1 teaspoon powdered ginger

1 teaspoon chilli powder

1 teaspoon cumin powder

30ml water, or enough to make a paste

Small bunch of coriander, chopped

1 lemon

30ml brown sugar

100ml water

For the tomatoes:

12 ripe vine tomatoes

1 teaspoon asafoetida

1 teaspoon mustard seeds

1 teaspoon cumin seeds

1 teaspoon salt

1 teaspoon turmeric

1 teaspoon chilli powder

1 teaspoon fresh ginger, grated

Method

For the rice: Soak basmati rice in a bowl of water for 20 minutes. Drain and put the rice in a pan.

Pour in enough clean water to just cover the rice, add a couple of bay leaves then bring to a gentle boil.

Place on the lid and turn off heat. Leave to stand for 15 minutes or until the water has evaporated and the rice is fluffy.

For the aubergine: Slice the aubergines in half lengthways and soak the slices in cold water to remove any bitterness.

Make a paste from the flour, ginger, chilli powder, cumin and coriander adding a bit of the water at a time until it becomes a smooth paste.

Rub over the aubergines and fry for 2 minutes each side. Add a dash of water to the pan, cover and steam for a further 5 minutes.

Squeeze on the lemon juice and scatter with brown sugar – add a little of the water to make a sauce and let it bubble and thicken for a further 5 minutes before serving.

For the tomato: Fry the asafoetida, mustard seeds, cumin seeds, salt, turmeric, chilli, fresh ginger and sugar in a deep frying pan or wok.

Add the tomatoes and gently combine with the spices.

Gently fry for 3-4 minutes, add a little water to make a sauce, toss and serve.

Serve with chopped red onion and tomato salad. Some natural yoghurt also gives it a bit of a buzz, but you can serve it with your favourite sides.

The chutney I used this time was a jar of local Yorkshire Red Onion Marmalade.

A group of INDIVIDUALS

All popular in their own right, The Forum Group has a fine collection of pubs, offering everything from great beers and spirits to amazing gastro delights.

The Forum Group may be Sheffield's largest independent bar and restaurant group, with seven venues under its umbrella, but there's plenty of individuality to be found at each establishment.

The Forum's been a cornerstone of Division Street for over 20 years since it was opened by restaurateur, and former international poster salesman, Kane Yeardley. It's been the catalyst for a wealth of bars and shops that have sprung up on the street – considered to be one of Sheffield's main independent hubs.

Upstairs is The Common Room, which has built a repuation as the city's trendiest sports bar and pool hall. The food offering pays homage to the American pit barbecue phenomenon and serves up chunky burgers, meat and more meat.

The Old House – based in what was once the Duke of Devonshire's town house – completes the Division Street trio. It's become especially known for its craft beers and range of gins, even running its own gin school – the best sort of education.

Further afield we have The York in Broomhill – a traditional pub with wholesome fare and a growing reputation for drink tasting evenings. Sister pub, The Broadfield on Abbeydale Road, has become Sheffield's favourite hang-out for pies – washed down with a pint of ale from their expansive range.

Heading out of the city, the Crown & Anchor in Barugh Green, Barnsley, is a breath of fresh air – offering local and international beers and a large garden to drink them in – whilst the British Oak at Mosborough, offers quirky décor and cosy nooks and crannies.

Steak
AND ALE PIE

We like to add a little pastry shape to our pie lids, a cow is our favourite for the steak pie. Serves 4-6

Ingredients

For the filling:

1kg beef flank or chuck, cut into small cubes

2 tablespoons vegetable oil

25g unsalted butter

2 tablespoons plain flour

2 teaspoons Henderson's Relish

300ml ale

300ml beef stock

12 whole shallots, peeled

2 large carrots, cut into chunks

1 tablespoon tomato purée

1 teaspoon dark brown sugar

Salt & pepper to season

For the pastry:

450g plain flour

100g strong bread flour

75g unsalted butter (cold)

200ml water

½ teaspoon salt

100g lard

1 beaten egg yolk (to glaze)

Method

Place the flour, salt and pepper in a large bowl. Add the chunks of beef and mix until coated evenly.

In a pan, heat one tablespoon of oil and the butter on a medium heat and brown the meat. Once sealed, transfer to a bowl.

In the same pan, add the carrots and shallots and sauté until they start to soften. Add more oil if needed.

Put the meat back in the pan, add the Hendo's and tomato purée and cook for another few minutes.

Pour in the ale and stock and bring to the boil.

Reduce the heat to a simmer and cover. Allow the meat to cook for another hour or until tender. Leave to cool and make your pie crust.

Place the plain flour and bread flour in a large bowl and mix.

Dice the butter into cubes about 1cm square. Add the butter to the flour and rub together with your fingertips.

In a large saucepan, combine the water, salt and lard and heat until just boiling.

Add to the flour mixture and mix together quickly with a wooden spoon.

Once it has cooled enough so you can touch the dough, ball it together and place on a lightly floured surface. Knead until smooth.

Your pastry should be ready to use now. Roll it out quickly (as the pastry cools it will become harder to work with).

Line your pastry tin, fill, and then cover with the remaining pie crust. You could use individual pie tins or one large tin.

Wash the beaten egg across the dough before cooking. This will ensure a nice golden colouring.

Bake for 35-40 minutes at 200°c until the pastry is golden. Leave to rest for 10 minutes before serving.

Foraging in the HEDGEROW

Forager and preserve maker Simon Ellis, journeys into the hedgerows to create some truly wonderful and imaginative jams and chutneys.

The call of the open road took its toll on former lorry driver and driving school owner Simon Ellis – so he turned his attention to the tastier side of life.

Simon launched The Hedgerow Preserving Company after seeing similar producers at Nether Edge farmers' market in 2011. Encouraged by friends and family who'd tasted the jams and chutneys he produced as a hobby, Simon booked a stall at the next market and got to work.

Without knowledge of mass production, he beavered away in his kitchen laboratory to create six chutneys, one jam and one marmalade to sell. They flew off the stall so quickly he decided to set up in business.

Simon's creations are more imaginative than your regular supermarket offerings. Rich flavours including damson and liquorice sauce (we tried this with duck and it was a perfect match), nettle beer mustard and caramelised carrot chutney form part of his range of over 70 products.

He loves to cook with more unusual ingredients such as medlar, and forages for plants including elderflower and nettles – gaining permission to pick them from land owners wherever he finds them growing.

Simon Ellis – A true 'from field to fork' entrepreneur.

Simon honed some of his foraging knowledge at a course run by Hartington's School of Food in Bakewell, led by experts Chris and Rose Bax from Taste the Wild – a company set up to promote wild food as exciting ingredients to use in innovative ways.

He was keen to enhance his understanding of the skill and found the day-long course taught him about ingredients he wasn't even aware of, such as sweet cicely – a weed to the untrained eye, but to those in the know its young leaves and seed pods boast a flavour similar to fennel.

Foraging is now an almost daily pastime for Simon, who still spends part of each week working as an advanced driving instructor. He's constantly on the lookout for fruits, shoots and leaves to include in his creations and is keen to expand on his local foraging knowledge – wild garlic and beech leaves are next on his list.

Ever the creative businessman, Simon has also founded his own 'crop swap', which encourages people to bring him surplus fruit and vegetables from their gardens and allotments in exchange for products from the Hedgerow collection.

Started in 2013, the crop swap grew from a conversation with a friend, who offered Simon horseradish from his garden any time he wanted it, in return for preserves. That sparked an idea and Simon started to approach local allotment growers about doing the same.

By word of mouth the crop swap began to grow and, in his first summer, Simon received 35 kilos of plums, 30 kilos of damsons, 20 kilos of medlars and 20 kilos of runner beans – as well as rhubarb, pumpkins, marrows and more. His freshest donation came from a customer at 'Beeley Handmade and Quirky' who liked the idea so much she went home, gathered redcurrants from her garden and brought them straight back.

Now stocked in a growing number of shops, including Porter Brook Deli and Welbeck Abbey Farm Shop, The Hedgerow Preserving Company is something to savour.

The cock o' THE NORTH

Not many foods become cultural icons, let alone inspire songs and works of art.
'Henderson's Relish' – Yorkshire's best kept secret.

Henderson's Relish may not yet be a household name across all parts of the UK – but in Sheffield it's both a cultural and culinary icon.

Created around 1885 by dry salter and wholesale druggist Henry Henderson, the spicy Yorkshire sauce was originally sold from his grocery shop in Broad Lane and gained immediate popularity.

It was almost lost to Sheffield in 1910 when Henderson sold the business to Shaw's of Huddersfield, a family firm producing pickles and vinegar. They moved production to better premises, which fortuitously remained in the city under the watchful eye of managing director Charles Hinkman.

Hinkman bought the business back from Shaw's in 1940 and became its chairman – a role he held until his death in 1953 when his sister Gladys took over. When Gladys died in 1981 her brother Harvey Freeman stepped in and the business has been passed down the Freeman line ever since. Its current head is Pamela, who took over from her late husband, Dr Kenneth Freeman, who was in charge from 1991-2013.

From 1960, Henderson's was produced at a site on Leavygreave Road – familiar to locals thanks to its red brick façade and bright orange signage. However, the business relocated in August 2013 to new premises just off Sheffield Parkway in order to be brought up to higher standards that would've proved too costly on the old site.

In over a century of production, Hendo's (as it's affectionately known) has been taken into Sheffielders' hearts. It's developed a cult following thanks to its strong, northern roots and mystique – the special recipe remains a well-kept secret.

The company's ability to have fun with its bottles has also been a factor in its success. Sheffield Olympian Jessica Ennis-Hill's gold medal victory was celebrated with gold labels stamped 'Congratulations Jessica, Strong and Northern', while rockers Arctic Monkeys celebrated the release of their AM album by bringing out 500 limited edition bottles – which sold out in minutes.

Labels for Sheffield United and Sheffield Wednesday fans have also been produced, as have charity editions for St Luke's Hospice, and commemorative tags for the likes of Warp Films and Sheffield United FC's 125th anniversary.

Adored by the masses, and with famous fans including Sheffield royalty Michael Palin, Sean Bean, Pete McKee, Richard Hawley and Arctic Monkeys, Hendo's is a good, traditional product with a history that's as rich and distinctive as its flavour.

Hendo's Man Flies Again
by Sheffield artist Luke Prest (www.lukeprest.com)

They've got SOLE, MANN

Brothers Christian & Danny have swam in culinary circles for more than two decades, but it's their passion for fishy things that really floats their boat.

Danny Szurko's day starts at 2:30am when he sets off to market. He handpicks a selection of whole fish to sell from J.H. Mann, the fishmongers he runs with brother Christian on Sharrowvale Road.

But theirs was not always a fishy business. Both accomplished chefs, their careers have seen them work in renowned London establishments such as The Ivy and J. Sheekey – the latter famous for its fish offering.

Children and family brought the brothers back to Sheffield in 2001. They worked at various restaurants in Sheffield and the Peak District until opening their own business, Lounge Bar, in the city centre in 2007.

Just three months into their venture, the Szurkos were approached by the daughter of Peter Mann, an old family friend who ran a fishmonger's shop in Hillsborough. He was looking to sell the business and, a matter of days later, Christian took the helm – leaving Danny to run the bar.

Eventually both brothers committed to J.H. Mann, an established name they chose to keep, closing the Hillsborough shop and opening a new one in Sharrow Vale in 2009.

This local jewel is home to a glittering oceanic display. Whole tuna, sea bass, hake, squid and snapper are laid out in all their glory alongside smoked eel, cured salmon and crustaceans.

Highly personal service, choice and quality are the offering here, with a litte education on the side... and plenty of sole!

Fresh
FISH &
GAME

Spiced
CURED SALMON

Ingredients

1 filleted side of very fresh salmon, weighing about 1kg

100g mixed baby salad leaves and extra virgin olive oil, to serve

For the salt mix:

300g coarse sea salt

400g caster sugar

3 star anise toasted and crushed

1 teaspoon coriander seeds toasted and crushed

1 teaspoon onion seeds

1 teaspoon fennel seed toasted and crushed

1 teaspoon chilli flakes

3 cloves garlic crushed

1 teaspoon tamarind paste

Zest 1 lime

Zest 1 lemon

Method

Tip all the ingredients for the salt mix into a large bowl, except the tamarind paste and mix well.

Stroke your hand along the salmon fillet to check for any stray bones. If you find any, pull them out with a pair of tweezers or small pliers.

Scatter about a third of the salt mix onto a large tray in a line about the size of the salmon fillet. Lay the salmon, skin-side down, take the tamarind paste and spread over the salmon (covering all gaps) then sprinkle over the rest of the salt mix on top. Cover with cling film, put another tray on top and weigh it down with a few cans. Leave in the fridge overnight or for at least 24 hrs.

If serving as a plated starter, use a sharp carving knife to cut the salmon straight down into fine slices, allowing 6 slices for each plate.

Squid
CURED SALMON

Ingredients

1 filleted side of very fresh salmon skin on, weighing about 1kg

For the salt mix

300g coarse sea salt

400g Demerara sugar

1 teaspoon coriander seeds toasted and crushed

1 teaspoon fennel seeds toasted and crushed

1 teaspoon chilli flakes

300g preserved lemon finely diced

½ lemon juiced and zest

50g squid ink

Method

Place the salmon flat, skin side down in a non-metallic container.

Place all the ingredients in a large bowl and give a good mix with a spatula (as the squid ink will colour your hand.)

Then spread the mixture over the salmon making sure everything is covered.

Cover with cling film and leave at room temp for 3-4 hours for the mixture to penetrate.

Place in your fridge for 2-3 days tipping any excess water out of the container from time to time.

To check if the cure is ready, gently press the salmon. Should be quite dense.

Slice on a slight angle and serve with a warm potato salad.

Meat the BUTCHERS

Expert butchers, John Crawshaw's, have built up a reputation for quality and consistency. Offering some of the finest meat in the region, as well as their award winning sausages, burgers and pies, delicious traditional cooked meats and dreamy home made cream cakes.

'Expert butchers for food lovers' is John Crawshaw's slogan. And thanks to the company's history, expertise and unrivalled quality there's no argument with that.

John Crawshaw's, founded in 1955 by John's father Brian, has grown from humble beginnings. It developed a strong identity thanks to its emphasis on producing high quality items of its own to add to an expanding range of fresh meat on offer.

The award-winning business developed its offering to include a wide variety of sausages, 'ready meals', home-cooked meats, sandwiches, pies and pastries – a fortuitous move that set them apart from supermarkets during the big food conglomerates' push on butchery in the '80s and '90s.

John Crawshaw's was able to flourish thanks to being able to offer better service, quality of product and variety of meats, which was enticing to customers.

Provenance is key, with much care and attention taken by John to personally select all the beef, pork and lamb for their

"Seven Hills" range, which is all sourced from local farms within 30 miles of the business. The highly skilled butchery team can produce any cut required to order, from traditional cuts such as brisket on the bone, to new favourites like bavette steaks.

Beef is matured on the bone, prior to butchery then vacuum packed and further matured for up to 6 weeks to enhance the flavour and tenderness of the meat.

John Crawshaw's dry-cured, rindless back and streaky bacon are best sellers and game is popular too with meat like venison, poussin and quail available for both the retail and catering markets to order.

Expansion has continued and the firm now has three retail stores, in Hillsborough, Chapeltown and Stocksbridge, and a new production kitchen facility alongside its successful catering arm, which supplies almost 150 outlets including restaurants, schools and hotels in and around Sheffield.

John Crawshaw's Butchers

Braised beef cheeks
WITH MASHED POTATO

This dish was prepared by Andy Gabbitas, at The Wortley Arms. Serves 4

Ingredients

4 John Crawshaw's beef cheeks

100ml red wine

1 tablespoon tomato purée

1 sprig thyme

2 bay leaves

100g flour

2 carrots

1 leek

1 celery

2 litres good beef stock

Method

Season with salt and pepper then seal the beef cheeks in a hot frying pan, remove and set to one side.

Finely chop the carrots, leek and celery and sweat gently in an oven proof pan until slightly translucent.

Add the flour and cook out slightly, then add the thyme, bay leaves, tomato purée and red wine to the pan and simmer gently for 5 minutes.

Add the beef cheeks back to the pan and cover with beef stock.

Place lidded in the oven at 150°c for 4 hours or until tender.

When done reduce and strain some of the sauce to make a gravy.

Serve with buttery mashed potato.

We're JAMMIN'

Matt Hulley may not be the king of rock and roll – but he certainly knows his onions, plums, peaches, oranges, apples, blackcurrants...

Despite a food marketing degree, and the conviction that his future lay in food, it took Just Preserves' owner Matt Hulley a while to hone his true calling.

A post-university customer services job in London didn't quite satisfy his appetite – so leaving the Big Smoke behind Matt pursued his calling and moved north to God's Own County.

Settling in Sheffield with partner Eve, he opened Hulley's Café in Ecclesall Road. Here, Matt felt a step closer to his dream, enjoying building a rapport with his customers. After 5 years of café life he looked to further refine his ambition.

Enter Keith and Heather Hoyland, preserve makers extraordinaire, based in Worrall on the outskirts of the city. Their expanding kitchen operation began as a hobby for the retired police workers but, with the preserves growing in popularity, the couple decided to retire and pass on their

mantle (and more importantly their secret recipes) in favour of a well-earned quiet life.

Matt initially worked alongside Keith, learning to cook the recipes in the Hoyland's kitchen, before moving to Just Preserves' purpose built kitchen unit on Chippinghouse Road.

Matt has expanded Just Preserves to supply over 35 local businesses and counting – with over 40 marmalades, jams, chutneys and pickles in the range.

The secret lies in cooking small batches, using a variety of natural ingredients sourced locally, and he still manages to produce up to an impressive 2,000 jars per month.

He now produces over 40 marmalades, jams, chutneys, and pickles – all from recipes learned from Keith and Heather.

Matt's next step? Refining the range and trying out some of his own recipes – while trying to keep up with demand.

Spicy sausage &
BEAN CASSEROLE

This hearty casserole from our friends at Snap Deli is best served with
something to mop up the delicious sauce. Try mashed potato or crusty bread.

Serves 4

Ingredients

2 tablespoons Just Preserves Hot
Tomato, Garlic & Chilli Relish

2 tablespoons olive oil

12 pork sausages (Pat O'Brien
butchers)

1 large white onion, chopped

1 bulb fennel, chopped

½ teaspoon fennel seeds

410g can cannellini beans (drained
and rinsed)

400g can chopped tomatoes

2 teaspoon brown sugar

Salt & pepper

Method

Heat the oil in a casserole dish over a medium heat and fry the sausages for 5 minutes,
turning often until they are browned all over. Remove from the pan and set aside.

Add the onion, fennel and fennel seeds to the pan and stir fry for approximately 5 minutes
until the onions and fennel are softened and coloured slightly.

Add the beans, tomatoes, Just Preserves relish and sugar to the pan and stir to combine.
Return the sausages to the pan and bring to the boil. Reduce the heat to a low simmer and
cook for 15 minutes or until the sausages are cooked through. Season to taste with salt and
pepper and serve with the side of your choice.

Vegetarian Option: Use herbed vegetarian sausages or a firm root vegetable like squash or
pumpkin in place of the pork sausages.

Butternut squash &
GOATS CHEESE TART

Snap Deli serve this as a lunchtime snack, but you can also have a more substantial dish by serving it with some chips & beans.

Serves 8

Ingredients

For the pastry:

250g plain flour

100g cold butter, cubed

50ml cold water (approximately)

For the filling:

150ml double cream

150ml milk

4 eggs (we use Aston Springs Farm)

1 large butternut squash

1 large red onion

125g log of goats cheese

100g Just Preserves chilli jam

Salt & pepper

Method

For the pastry:

Weigh out the flour and add a pinch of salt. Combine with the cubed butter, rubbing in with your fingertips until a breadcrumb consistency is achieved.

Gradually add water until a dough is formed. The pastry can be wrapped and chilled or frozen for up to a month.

Grease a 23cm loose bottomed tart case and dust with flour.

Pre-heat your oven to 180°c.

Roll out the pastry on a floured surface to a round slightly larger than your tart case. Roll it over your rolling pin and carefully place into your case. Don't worry about any overhanging pastry – as the pastry bakes it will shrink so these are trimmed afterwards.

Using a small ball of scrap pastry, shape the pastry round the edges of the tin. This stops any messy fingermarks on the case.

Place the case in the fridge to chill for 20 minutes.

Once chilled, prick the base all over with a fork. Line with baking parchment and fill with baking beans. Bake blind for 10-15 minutes.

Take out the beans and parchment and bake for a further 5-10 minutes until golden brown. Remove from the oven and allow to cool before trimming excess pastry by running a sharp knife around the edge of the tart case.

For the filling:

Peel the butternut squash, halve and remove the seeds with a spoon. Dice into chunks approximately 2cm cubed. Peel the onion and chop into large chunks.

Place into a roasting dish, drizzle with oil and lightly season with salt and pepper. Roast in the oven for 30-40 minutes until soft. Remove from the oven and drain off any excess oil.

Smear the bottom of your tart case with Just Preserves chilli jam and add the roasted vegetables. Tear the goats cheese into large chunks and arrange over the top.

To make the filling, whisk the eggs and combine with the milk and cream. Season well and fill the tart case.

Bake for 30-40 minutes until golden brown and set.

Chris Morgan's
FILLET BEEF WITH RED WINE JUS

Sheffield United legend Chris Morgan is a native of Barnsley ... but we'll not hold that against him. Having started his career with his hometown club, he moved to The Blades in 2003 – and has been there ever since. Holding positions as captain, assistant manager and caretaker manager at the club, you could say he's part of the furniture down at Bramall Lane.

As at home in the kitchen, as he is on the pitch, there's far more to Chris's culinary repertoire than a greasy chip butty. Serves 2

Ingredients

2 fillet steaks

2 chopped shallots

200ml red wine

1 sprig thyme

1 bay leaf

300ml good beef stock

Salt & freshly ground black pepper to taste

Knob of butter

Method

Season the fillets.

Pre-heat the oven to 180°c.

Heat a frying pan over medium high heat. Place steaks in a hot pan with a little oil, and seal on each side for 1 minute, or until browned. Place in the oven for 5 minutes for rare.

Pan-fry the shallots until caramelised, add the wine and herbs reduce by half, then add the stock and reduce by half again.

Strain through a sieve and bring back to boil. When all done, remove from heat and add butter

Season to taste.

Remove steaks to two warmed plates, drizzle round the sauce and serve immediately. We served ours with potato dauphinoise, a few mushrooms, bacon lardons and a herb dressing.

Born to be a
CAPOCUOCO

From his early days with a sweeping brush, to commanding the kitchen brigade, head chef Mario Cantelmi was born for this role – and you can tell.

Regional dishes from across Italy are the speciality of La Terrazza – a family-run restaurant that's built its reputation on authentic Italian cooking.

Founded in 1997 by Pasquale Cantelmi, the eatery has been a popular feature of Sharrowvale Road for nearly 2 decades.

Pasquale arrived in the UK in 1982 and has been running restaurants ever since. The restaurant is very much a family affair – with Pasquale's son Mario now head chef and Mario's wife Holly running front of house.

Mario has been part of the business since he was 10 years old – when he would help to mop up and polish cutlery after school. Mario became a chef at La Terrazza at 16 and by 17 had taken over full time.

Over the years, Mario has not only perfected his cooking skills, but also picked up his father's best tips on how to source fish and where to find the freshest produce. La Terrazza serves seafood from H Baldocks on Chesterfield Road and meat from Batty's in Woodseats. Other produce is also locally sourced.

Good quality, price and service is paramount for the Cantelmi's. All their desserts, bread, pizza dough, sauces and pesto are made on the premises, and their attention to detail has earned them a host of regulars. It's the place to be for a welcoming, laid-back atmosphere with friendly service and an authentic Italian experience.

Ravioli alla a'ragosta
CON SALSA DI GAMBERONI E 'NDUJA

Make the effort to find the 'Nduja, it's well worth it. The spicy salami paste adds some heat to the dish. This speciality artisan product comes from the Calabria region of Italy.

Ingredients

For the pasta:

200g Tipo 00 flour, plus extra for dusting

2 free range eggs

2 teaspoons olive oil

1 teaspoon salt (optional)

For the lobster:

Fresh lobster, enough for two people

20g fresh dill

10g tarragon

1 garlic clove, finely diced

100-150g breadcrumbs

1 tablespoon extra virgin olive oil

1 free range egg

50g parmesan cheese

For the sauce:

8 king prawns

Olive oil

1 clove garlic

10 pieces pepperoni salami

White wine

Fresh dill

Salt & pepper

200ml passata

100ml double cream

2 teaspoons 'Nduja (spicy salami paste)

Method

To make the pasta, tip the flour onto the work surface and make a crater shape.

Add the egg, salt and olive oil to the middle.

Slowly drag the flour into the wet mixture and combine with fingertips until well mixed together. If the dough seems too dry add tepid water a little at a time and knead until smooth. Be careful – the dough should not be too sticky.

Once ready, leave the dough under a damp cloth while you prepare the filling.

Dice the lobster tail and claw meat. Add to a bowl with the rest of the ingredients and mix thoroughly. Cover and leave in the fridge while preparing the pasta parcels.

Dust the work surface with flour and roll out the pasta dough into a square or rectangle 3mm thick.

Take the lobster from the fridge and spoon ¾ of a tablespoon of the mix an inch from the bottom corner of the dough. Repeat in a line leaving an inch of space between each spoonful.

Fold the top of the dough over to make a parcel and cut into individual parcels.

Place in the fridge until needed.

To make the sauce, pan fry the king prawns in olive oil and garlic.

Add the pepperoni salami and a touch of white wine.

Simmer gently and season with dill, salt and pepper to taste.

Add the passata and double cream then bring to a simmer.

Finally stir in the 'Nduja – add a little extra if it's to your taste.

To cook the pasta, put a tablespoon of vegetable oil, or salt if you prefer, into a pan of cold water and bring to the boil.

Add the ravioli one by one and cook for 4 minutes.

Pour the sauce over and serve.

A welcoming ATMOSPHERE

W.C. Fields famously said "I cook with wine, sometimes I even add it to the food." These are the sentiments of Frenchman-cum-Sheffielder, Patrick Jouan.

Stepping into the cool, dimly-lit interior of Le Bon Vin's wine shop is like entering a tranquil oasis, away from the bustle of everyday life.

Beautifully presented bottles line the walls, each one labelled by region, complete with a helpful, accessible description including grape varieties and characteristics for the wine novices among us.

But this is not an exclusive place. Knowledgeable, approachable staff offer a personal service to guide the buyer, making recommendations according to individual tastes and requirements. This creates Le Bon Vin's welcoming atmosphere – they're keen for people to pop in, taste the wines and feel at home.

French wines have a room to themselves, while wines from the rest of the world, including Tunisia, Lebanon and New Zealand occupy a neighbouring area.

The shop, founded by Frenchman Patrick Jouan and his wife Dianne, has been open for almost 20 years and the wholesale business almost 30.

They've built a reputation for quality, which is supported by their policy of choosing to source and sell single estate wines rather than the more common factory types. French cider, Champagnes, Prosecco and more unusual spirits are also available.

And, with bottles ranging from as little as £5.50 to over £250, there's something for everyone. Salut!

Patrick's PAIRINGS

Whites

Mission Estate Sauvignon Blanc, ABV 12.5%

Varieties: Sauvignon

Mission Estate Winery has unique historical significance in the development of New Zealand wine. Established in 1851, by the French Marist religious order, Mission Estate is the country's oldest winemaker.

This popular Sauvignon Blanc has a ripe bouquet of tropical fruits, citrus, passion fruit and gooseberry. The palate is crisp, fruity and dry with a clean lingering finish.

Enjoy with: Asian and Chinese food.

Domaine Saint Roch Les Demoiselles Touraine Sauvignon, ABV 12%

Varieties: Sauvignon

The Domaine Saint Roch is located in the small commune of Meusnes. Its vineyard, on the slopes above the village, grows vines on unique soil, imparting a gunflint-like flavour which gives its wines a unique, original character.

This Sauvignon has a powerful fragrance, a harmony of all the riches of its land with a delicate hint of muscatel.

Enjoy with: salmon, chicken, goat's cheese.

Domaine Leon Boesch 'Les Fous' Gewurztraminer, ABV 14.5%

Varieties: Gewurztraminer

Located in the commune of Westhalten in the heart of a natural reserve, Domaine Leon Boesch grows all its grapes without the use of chemicals.

Known in the region as the 'Emperor of Alsace', this wine is drier than many Gewurztraminers and has fragrant aromas and a distinctly piquant taste.

Enjoy with: spicy, aromatic food, like Indian cuisine.

Reds

Camille Cayran Secret de Campagne, ABV 13.5%

Varieties: Grenache Noir

This wine uses the very best grapes which are often harvested at night to preserve their freshness. The wine is light and peppery with a very light finish.

Enjoy with: stews and darker meat.

La Reserve du Maitre de Chais de Pizay Beaujolais, ABV 12.5%

Varieties: Gamay

Since the Middle Ages the fine wines of Chateau de Pizay have been appreciated by Beaujolais lovers. The magnificent 12th century chateau produces classic wines and regularly wins awards.

This wine is an excellent value Gamay embodying the best characteristics of the variety. It has a fruity, floral nose with red berry and blackcurrant notes and a light, fresh taste.

Enjoy with: charcuterie or a first course.

Chateau Haut Terrier Cotes de Bordeaux Blaye, ABV 13.5%

Varieties: Merlot, Cabernet

Originally established in 1850, the Chateau Haut Terrier was taken over by the Denechaud family in 1974 who continue to produce traditional wines in the spirit of the original winemakers of the region.

This wine is deep and intense in colour, with powerful fruit on the nose and plenty of soft tannins.

Enjoy with: red meat like lamb, or pork.

All of the wines above are priced in the £7-£17 range.

Paradise FOUND

The Peak District National Park is one of our region's greatest assets. Chef Darren Goodwin is using the abundance of great ingredients on his doorstep to create some truly astounding dishes.

Losehill House is the only four star hotel in the Peak District National Park.

A blend of Arts & Crafts character and contemporary chic, it was built in 1914 as a country retreat for walkers and was popular until 2001 when the foot and mouth outbreak forced its closure and it fell into dereliction.

The building was given a new lease of life when it was converted into a hotel and ran as a low key operation until experienced hoteliers Paul and Kathryn Roden took it over in 2007.

Refurbished to high standards, Losehill now boasts a spa and a Michelin-recommended restaurant alongside its en-suite rooms.

Head chef Darren Goodwin's passion is fine dining and his daily changing menus mean the food is constantly evolving. Dishes are created from what's seasonally available at market, meaning absolute freshness with plenty of creative flair and eye-catching, precise presentation.

Rhubarb and a handful of herbs are grown on site, while eggs, milk, other herbs and honey are sourced a stone's throw away at Bennetts, Middletons Dairy, The Herb Table and The Sheffield Honey Company respectively.

The beautiful Orangery Restaurant, with its spectacular views of the surrounding countryside, ensures that Losehill truly offers an unforgettable experience.

Losehill House

Photo courtesy of Symbiosis Design

Ox cheek
CELERIAC & SPINACH LASAGNE

Serves 4

Ingredients

To braise the ox cheek:

2 x 300g ox (beef) cheeks dusted with a little flour

A splash of oil for frying

1 onion

2 carrot

½ bulb garlic

A few sprigs of thyme

1 litre beef stock or brown chicken stock

For the ragu:

1 glass red wine

200ml passata

For the celeriac lasagne sheets:

1 celeriac

100ml white wine vinegar

100g sugar

2 peppercorns

250g baby spinach leaves. Washed and any big stalks picked off

25g butter

Freshly grated nutmeg

Method

Pre-heat the oven to 150°c.

Brown the cheek in a casserole dish and add the roughly chopped vegetables. When they are browned add the stock. Make sure the cheeks are covered then place a lid on the dish or cover with foil.

Place the dish in the oven for around 2 hours and 30 minutes until the meat is tender.

Lift the meat out and shred it into a bowl using two forks. Strain the stock and reserve (skim off any fat as it settles on top).

In a fresh pan reduce the red wine and passata. When reduced by half, add the shredded meat and the reserved cooking stock and reduce until a thick sauce is achieved. Add salt and pepper as required.

Wash and peel the celeriac and slice thinly into 1mm thick sheets – you could use a large round cutter for neat circles.

Heat the sugar, vinegar and peppercorns until the sugar has dissolved. Add the celeriac sheets to the pickling liquid and leave for 5 minutes or until the celeriac begins to soften.

Wilt the spinach in a pan with a small knob of butter over a gentle heat. Season with salt and a little grated nutmeg.

To serve:

Ensure each component is still hot and layer up the ox cheek ragu, celeriac slices and wilted spinach. Use the round cutter to keep the lasagne in a neat stack.

Heart & soul
OF THE CITY

Racing team manager Mat Frolish may have swapped the track for the tea trolley, but with Lynne's recipes at the heart of the business – he's racing ahead.

Lynne's Pantry is a Sheffield gem. Founded in 1978 it's one of the city's oldest cafés, tucked away amid Surrey Street's cobbles.

Lynne Frolish, who set up the business, was a natural cook and her fresh, homemade food – complemented by her infectious, bubbly personality and vivacious character – soon gained her a wealth of regulars. And a husband.

She met Graham, a relative of the café's previous owners, the day she opened the shop. The fates conspired and the couple married just 5 months later.

Lynne worked tirelessly to build the cafe's solid reputation, pouring her heart and soul into the business. Cream teas, scones and pork sandwiches (which some claim are the best in the city) are as popular now as they were when she embarked on her venture. A second shop followed in June 2003 close to the city's busy hospital and universities.

Sadly, Lynne lost a long battle with cancer in 2012, and the pantry is now run by her son, Mathew, a former motorsport employee, with input from his father.

Good, hearty, traditional food is still at the core of the business – with much of it sourced locally. Pollards coffee has been used since day one, with fresh baked bread coming from Alf Turner Bakers for over 20 years. Meat is sourced from John Crawshaw's and veg from Webb's.

They also offer a delivery service, and corporate lunches, with plans to expand the business further – Lynne's legacy is sure to live on.

Lynne's Pantry

Lynnie's
FAMOUS SCONES

We serve these in a Yorkshire Cream Tea, which includes roast beef and pork
sandwiches, with a pot of tea and my mom's famous scones.
You can adjust the quantity to suit – or be generous and treat friends and family.
Makes 20 using a medium cutter.

Ingredients

800g self-raising flour

400g margarine or butter

400g sugar

225g sultanas

7 large eggs

¾ of a pint of milk

Method

Rub the margarine or butter into the flour and sugar to resemble fine breadcrumbs, then add the sultanas. Whisk the eggs and milk together and then add to the dry ingredients – but reserve enough to glaze prior to baking.

Take a shallow roasting tin (approx 1" high in depth) and grease well with margarine. Cut out the scones using a 3" diameter cutter and place in the tin with scones touching and slightly pushed together (this helps them to rise nice and high). Glaze with the egg and milk mix.

Bake in a hot oven at 220°c for 15-20 minutes or until golden brown.

Cut into nice big squares and serve with best butter or jam & cream.

New York GLAMOUR

The addition of chef Marco Pierre White to the Sheffield food scene is seen by many as a massive step forward for the city and a giant leap for food-kind...

A little New York glamour arrived in Sheffield in 2014 – with the opening of the city's first 'big name' celebrity chef restaurant by Marco Pierre White.

Located on the site of the former West Bar police station, adjoining Sheffield's new Hampton by Hilton hotel, the 90-cover family-friendly restaurant offers something for everyone.

The American-Italian inspired menu features dishes including pasta, pizza, steaks and seafood and also offers a dedicated children's menu. Head chef John Cluckie, who's lived in Sheffield for over a decade, has given the menu a local flavour by sourcing meat from butcher Owen Taylor and beers from Kelham Island Brewery.

Walls and furnishings in neutral shades of stone and taupe sit alongside impressive bonsai trees and a shining open kitchen pass – making the restaurant interior a classy yet welcoming space.

The long bar and lounge offer plenty of space for a relaxing drink – with choices ranging from an array of signature cocktails to a diverse wine and drinks list.

Marco's is a place where celebrity style comes as standard – whether diners are enjoying a bite after work, dinner with the family, or getting dressed up for a special night and enjoying quality food.

Marco's New York Italian

Roast rump of lamb
WITH FIVE BEAN CASSOULET

Serves 4

Ingredients

4 rumps of lamb (200-225g)

1 large white onion, diced

3 cloves of garlic, finely sliced

1 bay leaf

2 peeled carrots, diced

3 peeled sticks of celery, diced

200g butter beans, drained

200g garbanzo beans, drained

200g kidney beans, drained

200g cannellini beans, drained

200g borlotti beans, drained

2 sprigs rosemary

1 litre lamb stock

500g chopped tomatoes

Seasoning

Method

In a large pan, add a touch of olive oil and sweat off the vegetables and garlic on a medium heat until soft and colourless.

Add the bay leaf and rosemary and cook for 1 minute to infuse. Add the beans, chopped tomatoes and stock, reduce the heat and leave to simmer approximately 90 minutes until it starts to thicken. Season with salt and pepper to taste.

Pre-heat the oven to 180°c about 30 minutes before you are ready to start cooking the lamb. Season the lamb with salt and pepper and heat a roasting tray with oil on top of the stove. Add the lamb and seal all over till brown. Place in the middle of the oven and roast for 15-20 minutes depending on how you like your lamb cooking. Remove from the oven and allow to rest for at least 8 minutes.

Pour the juices from the meat in to the bean mix and stir. Warm four bowls and add some of the bean mix. Slice the lamb in to five or six slices and lay on top and drizzle with extra virgin olive oil.

We suggest serving with boiled new potatoes.

The tradtional & CONTEMPORARY

Set in the beautiful surroundings of the Derwent Valley. The Maynard is a mixture of traditional and contemporary in perfect harmony.

The Maynard may be known locally as a beautiful wedding venue and boutique hotel, but it also boasts one of the area's best restaurants.

The two AA Rosette eatery overlooks the historic building's landscaped garden and the valley beyond – providing a picturesque backdrop for diners.

The head chef and his team have built The Maynard's reputation for food on consistency of quality, flavour and presentation. Cooking fresh produce is our kitchen brigade's passion and they take great inspiration from the seasons.

Highlights of his menu range from grilled venison and roast rare breed Dexter beef, to whole roast sea bass and smoked chicken & tarragon terrine.

Local firms such as Middleton Dairy, The Herb Table and Country Fresh Foods supply the kitchen's fresh ingredients

– complementing a daily changing menu. Drinkers can also enjoy local fare with guest beers from the likes of Peak Ales and Abbeydale Brewery.

More local influence is present in original artwork adorning The Maynard's walls. Traditional sits alongside contemporary with works by Peter Hill, Kristan Baggaley and Steve Mehdi – whilst the cutlery is from Hathersage-based David Mellor.

During the 1938 cricket tour for 'The Ashes' the Australian touring party, featuring legendary batsman Donald Bradman, used The Maynard as their base for some of the northern tests. Reputedly they matched their on-field exploits with some less well-documented mischief off-field as well.

Combine all this with a longstanding, friendly team, and The Maynard's restaurant promises the ultimate dining experience – with the best of food, setting and service.

Corned beef terrine

WITH CELERIAC REMOULADE AND FIG & APPLE BREAD

Serves 12

Ingredients

For the corned beef terrine:

1-1.5kg beef brisket

100g table salt

Enough cold water to cover

20ml Brock & Morten Derbyshire rapeseed oil

2 large carrots, peeled and roughly chopped

1 large brown onion, roughly chopped

4 sticks celery, roughly chopped

1 leek, roughly chopped

100ml Henderson's Relish

4 pints good quality beef stock

1 pint Abbeydale Brewery Moonshire Pale Ale

1 teaspoon sea salt

2 teaspoons cracked black pepper

2 teaspoons ground mace

For the bouquet garni:

2 fresh bay leaves

4 sprigs fresh thyme

1 sprig fresh rosemary

10 parsley stalks (reserving the leaves for later)

For the celeriac remoulade:

1 head celeriac, peeled and grated

2 teaspoons nigella or black onion seeds

3 teaspoons parsley, chopped

4 tablespoons crème fraiche

2 tablespoons mayonnaise

For the fig & apple bread:

360g strong white bread flour

20g salted butter

15g fresh baker's yeast

¼ teaspoon table salt

¼ teaspoon caster sugar

110ml warm water

110ml milk

25g dried figs, finely chopped and soaked in the warm water

1 Granny Smith apple, grated with the skin on

Method

For the corned beef terrine:

Soak the brisket in the salt water solution for 24 hours then rinse under cold running water for 20 minutes. Discard the salt water solution.

Lighlty saute the carrots, onion, celery and leek in the rapeseed oil, then add the brisket, bouquet garni, beef stock, pale ale, Henderson's and seasoning. Bring slowly to the boil and reduce to a gentle simmer.

Put the lid on the pot and cook for approximately 6-8 hours. If the liquid level drops and the brisket is not covered, top up with water.

Check that the brisket is cooked by inserting a skewer – you will get very little resistance from the meat when ready. Remove the pan from the heat and let it cool.

Remove the brisket from the cooking liquor, reserving two pints for later. Flake the meat into strands and place in a bowl while still warm.

Add the chopped parsley leaves and two teaspoons of ground mace and mix thoroughly.

Take the two pints of reserved cooking liquor, add 50ml Henderson's Relish and reduce on the stove by half. When reduced pour over the flaked brisket and mix thoroughly again.

Line a terrine mould or a 2lb loaf tin with a double layer of cling film, making sure there is a sufficient overhang to cover the top of the terrine.

Spread the brisket mix evenly throughout the mould, fold over the cling film to cover, then find a suitable weight to place on top. Leave in the fridge overnight to press.

For the celeriac remoulade:

Thoroughly mix all the ingredients and add salt and freshly ground pepper to taste. Set aside in the fridge until ready to serve.

For the bread:

Mix the warm water, soaked figs, milk and yeast together then leave to rest for 10 minutes.

Meanwhile, mix together the flour, salt, sugar, butter and grated apple.

Gradually add the yeast mix and bring together using a mixer or spoon.

Leave the mix to rest somewhere warm in a bowl covered in cling film until nearly doubled in size.

Grease and flour a 1lb loaf tin if making a loaf.

Knock back the bread dough, kneading for about 10 minutes then either shape into small bread rolls or place in the prepared loaf tin.

Leave to prove again for 30 minutes.

Bake in the oven at 160°c for 30 minutes as a loaf or 15-20 minutes as rolls.

These are best served warm so do this as close to serving as possible.

To serve:

Take the terrine out of the fridge 15 minutes before serving as it will benefit from being served slightly warmer. Slice the corned beef into 1cm thick pieces.

Serve with a dollop of the celeriac remoulade or for neatness place in a ring mould and arrange the terrine around it.

Warm the bread through the oven if made prior to serving and accompany with some good quality salted butter.

Going the EXTRA MILE

Hailed by many as one of the finest restaurants in the North,
The Milestone has the culinary crowd all a flutter.

The future of this much-loved gem in Kelham Island's culinary crown was very nearly jeopardised by the floods of 2007 – just six months after owner Matt Bigland opened.

From early foundations as a sports bar, serving up pizza and tapas, The Milestone has evolved into a gastro pub with culinary flare – boosted by the acclaim of being named Gordon Ramsay's Best British Restaurant in 2010.

The Milestone team has since honed its identity to become a Sheffield favourite with strong, gutsy food, local sourcing and nose-to-tail cooking using every part of the animal – an education for staff and diners alike.

Matt sees The Milestone's future in pursuing these channels further still and continuing to think outside the box.

The team is passionate about incorporating local landscapes and nature into dishes by foraging for fresh herbs and serving locally-shot game.

Being selective and providing outstanding quality is top of their priority list, as well as introducing more unusual cuts to their customers in new, exciting ways.

And that includes a DIY approach to good food. The Milestone is passing on some of its secrets to diners via an increasingly popular cookery school – which runs courses on everything from bread making and knife skills to butchering and cooking your own pig.

Yorkshire rhubarb
WITH YOGHURT & COX'S APPLE

Ingredients

For the compressed apple:
5 Cox's apples

2g ascorbic acid

For the apple syrup:
500g freshly juiced Cox's apples

250g unsalted butter, finely cubed and chilled

550g refined caster sugar

10g yellow pectin

For the caramelised apple pastel:
375g reserved apple syrup

135g water

5g malic acid

6g yellow pectin

25g refined caster sugar

For the rhubarb compressing liquor:
500g grenadine

500g rose Champagne

For the rhubarb purée:
500g rhubarb, finely sliced

175g rhubarb juice

75g rhubarb compressing liquor

For the rhubarb emulsion:
250g rhubarb purée

90g unsalted butter, finely cubed & chilled

35g compressing liquor

For the compressed rhubarb:
500g rhubarb

250g compressing liquor

For the rhubarb sorbet:
250g rhubarb purée

50g caster sugar

50g water

50g compressing liquor

25g liquid glucose

2.5g stabiliser

For the aerated rhubarb yoghurt:
400g Greek yoghurt

35g Sosa Pro Espuma cold

1g citric acid

Seeds of 1 fresh vanilla pod

100g rhubarb purée

For the pearl spelt and oats:
100g pearl spelt

25g oats

Muscovado sugar

Sea salt

For the rhubarb jelly:
250g rhubarb juice

2g agar agar

3.5 sheets of gelatine

Caster sugar

Method

For the compressed apple:
Whisk the acid into 500g of cold water to dissolve.

Peel the apples and reserve the peelings. Using a melon baller, scoop balls from each apple and place them into the acidulated water. Reserve the excess apple.

Pass the excess apple through a juicer, remove the apple balls from the water and place in a vacuum bag with the fresh apple juice and place the bag in a vacuum chamber to -1 Bar. Reserve until needed.

For the apple syrup:
Mix the pectin with 50g of the sugar and reserve until needed.

Caramelise the remaining sugar. Gradually whisk the butter into the caramel to emulsify, then repeat this process with the apple juice. Whisk in the pectin mixture and boil for 2 minutes, pass through a fine chinois and reserve until needed.

For the caramelised apple pastel:
Line a 19x10cm dessert frame tightly with cling film and place on a chopping board, keep in the fridge until needed.

Mix the pectin and sugar, set aside.

Mix the malic acid with 10g of water, set aside.

Combine the remaining water and apple syrup and bring to the boil. Whisk in the pectin mixture and heat to 108°c. Remove from the heat and whisk in the acidulated water.

Pour into the prepared dessert frame, leave at room temperature for 12 hours to set, cut into 1 inch cubes and reserve at room temperature until needed.

For the rhubarb compressing liquor:
Combine and reserve until needed.

For the rhubarb purée:
Place all of the ingredients in a Thermomix and blend for 15 minutes at 80°c, pass through a fine chinois, cool over ice and reserve until needed in the fridge.

For the rhubarb emulsion:
Place the purée and liquor in a Thermomix and heat to 60°c. Gradually add the cubes of butter until completely emulsified, cool over ice and reserve until needed in the fridge.

For the compressed rhubarb:
Cut the rhubarb into 2cm pieces, place in a vacuum bag with the liquor and place in a vacuum chamber to -1 Bar. Place the sealed bag in a water bath heated to 88°c for 6 minutes, remove the bag and immediately place in iced water to cool. When cool, reserve in the fridge until needed.

For the rhubarb sorbet:
Gently heat all of the ingredients together until they have all dissolved, around 70°c.

Cool the mixture in a bowl over ice, then churn in an ice cream machine. Reserve in an airtight container in the freezer at -18°c until needed.

For the aerated rhubarb yoghurt:
Blend the ingredients together, pass through a fine chinois. Place in a siphon and charge with 1 N2o cartridge. Refrigerate for 2 hours before using.

For the pearl spelt and oats:
Wash the spelt under cold running water for 10 minutes, then place in a pan and cover with cold water. Simmer until the spelt has absorbed the water and is soft. Toss under cold running water again for 1 minute and pat dry.

Place on a baking sheet and dehydrate in the oven at 60°c for 12 hours. Cool it to room temperature and then deep fry in vegetable oil at 220°c for a few seconds until it has puffed up and it goes crispy.

Remove from the oil and toss in a little muscovado sugar to season it, followed by the salt.

Gently toast the oats until golden and mix through the puffed spelt. Cool and reserve in an airtight container until needed.

For the 'apple tree twigs and leaves':
Place the reserved apple skins on a baking sheet and dehydrate in the oven at 60°c for 12 hours, until dried and crispy. Reserve in an airtight container until needed.

For the rhubarb jelly:
Bloom the gelatine in cold water.

Slowly simmer the rhubarb juice, season with the sugar to taste. Add the agar agar whilst blending the hot solution for 2 minutes with a handheld blender. Remove from the heat, squeeze out any excess water from the gelatine and gradually stir in to the liquid.

Pass through a fine chinois into a 10x10cm container lined with bake spray. Chill to 4°c then carefully remove the jelly and cut into cubes. Reserve in the fridge until needed.

WI Member Jennifer Marsden's
VICTORIA SPONGE

Seven Hills Women's Institute member and HR consultant, Jennifer Marsden, chose a classic Victoria Sponge for her recipe.

Jennifer says; 'A Victoria sponge was one of the first cakes I remember making. It's also the cake I baked for Seven Hills WI's inaugural meeting. After all, it's something of a classic within the women's institute!'

She added, 'I've deviated a little and used Damson jam for this recipe. This jam is one of my favourites made by a local company called Hedgerow Preserves. I've also used cream as I like my cakes to be moist. It had to be proper whipping cream rather than butter cream though!'

Seven Hills Women's Institute has a whopping 135 members – making it the largest WI in the area. They're a group of self-confessed foodies and their annual stall at the Sheffield Food Festival has raised thousands of pounds for charity over the last 3 years.

Ingredients

For the cake:

220g caster sugar

220g softened unsalted organic butter, plus a little for greasing

4 free range organic eggs, beaten

220g self-raising flour, sifted

1 teaspoon baking powder

2 tablespoons milk (if desired)

For the filling:

Whipped double cream

Jar of Hedgerow Preserves Damson Jam

Icing sugar, to decorate

Method

Heat the oven to 180°c then grease two 20cm sandwich tins. Line the bottom with baking paper and dust the sides lightly with flour. In a mixing bowl, cream the butter and sugar until light and fluffy. Beat the eggs into the mixture, a little at a time, and fold in the sifted flour and baking powder. Add milk if required so the mixture has a dropping consistency.

Divide the mixture evenly between the tins then smooth with a spatula. Place the tins in the middle of the oven and bake for 20-25 minutes until golden and coming away from the edge of the tin. Using a clean finger, gently test that the cake springs after being pressed.

Set the cakes aside to cool for 5 minutes then run a knife around the edge of the tins. Carefully turn onto a cooling rack and leave to cool completely.

Place one of the cakes onto a clean plate and spread on a layer of jam. Top with the whipped cream and place the second cake on top.

Dust with a little icing sugar before serving. Keep in an airtight container and eat within 2 days.

It's the family BUSINESS

Often referred to as 'the drinks departmental store' Mitchell's is a family business with enough Sheffield heritage to fill this whole book – and that's before you talk about their fabulous range of wines, spirits, beers and cigars.

The History

Mitchell's is a family business steeped in Sheffield history.

Started by the late Dennis Mitchell in 1935, Mitchell's became an off licence in 1964 and was taken over by his son John, its current owner. John's late wife Diana worked for the business until her untimely death in 1999 and John has been joined in recent years by his daughter Francesca.

The drinks industry is in the family's blood. Dennis was born above the Waggon & Horses, Millhouses, in 1917 – one of several pubs in the Sheffield area run by John's grandfather Harry.

He managed the Middlewood Tavern; (pictured opposite top left) this picture is from 1922, he then took on the George IV on Infirmary Road until 1933 – a pub frequented by the infamous Mooney Gang who controlled Sheffield's gambling ring.

When Dennis reached school age, Harry elected to send him to Henry Fanshawe Grammar at Dronfield. Dennis left at 16 to work for Dewhurst butchers and went on to open Mitchell's butchers in the newly developed Meadowhead housing estate he'd noticed on his route to school.

But Sheffield lifeblood runs deeper still in the Mitchell family. One notable ancestor was Joseph Mitchell (1727-1788) who married Mary Boulsover, daughter of Sheffield Plate inventor Thomas Boulsover (1705-1788).

Another was John's great grandfather, Henry Sampson, who ran the Adelphi hotel from 1844-1867. The Adelphi was the place where three major sports teams were founded: Yorkshire County Cricket Club in 1863, Sheffield Wednesday in 1867 and Sheffield United in 1889. The building was demolished in 1969 to make way for the Crucible theatre.

Other notable family members include John Brightmore Mitchell, a prominent architect who designed, built and lived in Parkhead Hall and passed away in 1895, and William Brightmore Mitchell who married Louis Hodgson. Her father, Dr. Hodgson, built the Bell Hagg Inn – which was known locally as Hodgson's Folly. Furthermore, Mary Elizabeth Mitchell married Thomas Masterson in 1832, – he won a medal at the Battle of Waterloo and is listed as a Chelsea pensioner.

Present Day

Mitchell's is a departmental wine store like no other.

It's an Aladdin's cave – with over 900 different wines, 500 malt whiskies, 100 English bottled beers and a vast selection of handmade cigars.

John has poured 50 years of experience and passion into the business. He believes the key to Mitchell's success is the right products at the right price – sold by knowledgeable staff. They offer a friendly, personal service, to each and every customer.

And if it's a drink you're looking for, if you can't get it at Mitchell's – you can't get it anywhere.

Mitchell's Wine Merchants

Wine

With a vast array of wines to choose from, Mitchell's wine department offers the perfect taste and style to pair with any dish you cook.

John has tips for eating out too: "This book is full of fabulous restaurants, run by brilliant chefs, offering amazing food – and knowing which wine to pick when you're dining out can be tricky," he says. "My biggest rule of thumb when choosing wine to match food is to drink what you enjoy. However, here are some suggestions…"

Beef – Cabernet Sauvignon

First choice, Red Bordeaux Haut Medoc. Great tannins, full flavoured blackcurrant, cedarwood and tobacco, oak aged, often blended.

Lamb – Shiraz/Syrah

First choice, Northern Rhone Hermitage. Powerful, peppery with spice, full bodied, tannin and moreish.

Curry – Riesling

First choice, Alsace. Fresh & fruity, aromatic, slightly perfumed, high acidity and found in the best Indian restaurants.

Pasta/Lasagne – Barbera

The only choice, Italian Barbera. Robust red intense fruit and enhanced tannic content, fresh blackberries go fantastically with spaghetti bolognese.

Chicken – Chardonnay (Unoaked)

First choice, Chile. Temperature controlled in steel tanks creates lemon, lime citrus flavours, green skinned grapes.

Shellfish – Albarino

The only choice, Spain, Galicia. Known as Alvarinho in Portugal but the Spanish style offers distinctive aromas of apricot and peach with light acidity is superb.

Fish – Sauvignon Blanc

First choice, Marlborough, New Zealand, Tropical fruits, herbaceous and grassy, the NZ version is pure gooseberries.

Whisky

In the early '70s, Mitchell's was the first shop in Yorkshire to stock over 100 different malt whiskies. Today it offers a fabulous range of nearly 500 different malts and whiskies from around the world.

John is a firm believer in whisky ratings by Jim Murray in his Whisky Bible. Murray claims whiskies rating 98-100 are better than anything he has ever tasted and that 94-97.5 are superstar whiskies that give us a reason to live.

Ardbeg Uigeadail – 97.5 points. From Islay this is your peaty one, massive yet tiny, loud yet whispering.

Old Pultney 21 Year – 97.5 points. Northern Highlands and one of the great undiscovered distilleries. The most delicate smoke imaginable, salt & spices absolutely exploding from the glass. World Whisky of the Year 2012.

Amrut Fusion – 97 points. India, one of the most complex and intriguing new whiskies of 2010.

Powers Johns Lane – 96.5 points. Irish, this 12-year-old is unmistakable, utopian. Pure Irish but still embracing and magnificent, one of the world whiskies of the year.

Highland Park 18 Year – 95.5 points. Orkney Isles, a thick dollop of honey spread across a layer of salted butter with eye closing beauty.

Glenfarclas 105 – 95.5 points. Speyside, dynamic. No other Sherry Cask finish is full of the joys of Jerez.

St George Chapter 7 – 94 points. English, rum finish, distilled in March 2007 and bottled in October 2010, absolutely exceptional. The youth of this malt and the sweet finesse of the rum casks were born for each other.

Mackmyra First Edition – 93.5 points. Sweden, Swedish oak, knee weakening like being whipped by a busty blonde dominatrix (or so a judge friend of mine tells me).

Penderyn Sherrywood – 93 points. Wales, oak and sherry and absolutely dry, this proves that the Welsh can produce exceptional whiskies.

Longrow cv – 91 points. Campbeltown, J&A Mitchell – but sadly not my distillery – nippy spices, smoked with a dry tobacco edge, the nose and delivery is something special.

Beer

"I may be a wine merchant, but I've always loved a beer," admits John. "The first I ever had was a bottle of Double Diamond – so, in this thirsty world, we're looking for beers that raise the bar."

He takes up the story...

Sheffield is noted as the beer capital of the UK thanks to the still-growing number of micro breweries – which are sending our taste buds into orbit.

The success we've had with our local friends has been fantastic, but we've also scoured Yorkshire and surrounding regions for some more great beers.

Nearby Bradfield Brewery, based on a busy working farm, has had phenomenal success with Farmers Blonde, while Bakewell's Thornbridge Brewery has won many awards with its Jaipur, 5.9% India Pale Ale, which is massively hoppy with accentuated honey.

Kelham Island Brewery, built in 1990 in the beer garden of the Fat Cat on Alma Street, was started by my late good friend Dave Wickett – whose enthusiasm pushed the growth of the real ale movement and inspired a generation of new small breweries.

We also stock bottles from Sheffield's Wood Street Brewery (WSB), Acorn at Barnsley, Wentworth at Rotherham and Welbeck Abbey – whose head brewer Claire Monk is one of the few female brewers in the country.

A little further afield is Durham Brewery, with a wonderful range of bottle-conditioned beers including a 10% Russian Stout – no wonder it's called Temptation. Cloister is their Premium Bitter and they also have a 7.2% White Stout.

From West Yorkshire we have Saltaire Brewery. Amongst the range is Raspberry Blonde (I think I went out with her once). There's also a Triple Chocoholic which has a great hoppy flavour with a chocolate bitter finish and has won two international gold medals.

Wold Top from the Yorkshire Wolds near my beloved Bridlington do two gluten-free beers: Scarborough Fair India Pale Ale and Against the Grain, which is recommended by the Coeliac Society.

"Where 'as tha been since I saw thee?" Well, how about Ilkley Brewery? And its lovely little number packed with American hops called Mary Jane at 3.5% – a fantastic session ale.

Little Valley Brewery from Hebden Bridge is 100% organic and vegan approved. The hops and malts go hand-in-hand with our great soft Yorkshire water and all the beers are bottle conditioned.

If you fancy a treacle stout look no further than Ossett Brewery. I'm a brunette man but they do a lovely Yorkshire Blonde – full bodied, well rounded and sweet on the palate.

Up in North Yorkshire we have Copper Dragon from Skipton. My two favourites are Scotts 1816, which is distinctively hoppy, and Golden Pippin – a light refreshing blond with a citrus fruit flavour.

Last but not least, Sam Smith's (which we have sold forever) is now all vegan and vegetarian approved.

All these fantastic breweries have filled the gap left by the loss of Sheffield Whitbreads in 1993, Hope & Anchor in 1994 and Stones & Wards in 1999. Sheffield's beer future is bright.

Cigars

There's nothing better than an hour's smoke courtesy of a fat Cuban cigar.

Mitchell's walled humidor holds over 100 different types of fine Havana cigars, which puts them in the North's top 3 leading 'Cigar Specialists Gold Standard.'

Mitchell's Wine Merchants

Moor to the MARKET

The jewel in Sheffield's crown is the amazing market building situated on The Moor – a diverse and exciting mix of food and cultures fit to grace any city and already being referred to as 'the Borough Market of the north'.

A new era began in Sheffield at the end of 2013 when the Moor Market opened its doors for the first time.

Drawing over a million customers in the first three months, the £18 million market brought a new lease of life to the Moor area of the city centre – especially with its food offering.

A plethora of fresh fruit, vegetables, fish and meat traders have taken up residence in the dynamic new building, which boasts a unique design combining a timber 'diagrid' frame and sleek glass frontage.

The market's bustling, friendly atmosphere hits you the moment you step inside.

It's rare not to find a queue outside Waterall Brothers butchers – their pork pies, which are freshly made every day, are deemed worth the wait. Nearby are the doughy delights of artisan bakery Seven Hills, offering a variety of staple and enriched breads from wholemeal, white and rye to apricot and hazelnut sourdough.

Wind your way between the stalls and you'll find S&J's Pantry selling, among other items, a range of specialist cheeses, with more to be found at Dearne Farm Foods' outlet alongside meat, eggs and other dairy products.

Fishmongers including Smith & Tissington and Bingham's provide an oceanic offering of seafood, shellfish and crustaceans, while nuts, spices and olives can be found a stone's throw away at The Nut Bar and Green Leaves.

Plenty of additional specialist items can be found on the market's stalls, including gluten free options, goat's meat, goose eggs and golden beetroot. Beer Central, the specialist craft beer shop, offers a treasure trove of local and global tipples, while greengrocer stalls are studded with exotic jewels such as pomelo, mooli, plantain and okra.

Hungry shoppers can take a break and dine in the food court area. Tastebuds can be taken on a global journey with outlets serving British, Cossack, Italian and Asian cuisine. Maybe adhere to tradition with an all-day breakfast or tuck in to some tasty steak and ale pie. For a lighter bite you can grab a sandwich or healthy salad.

Fantastic choice and value aside, personal service and extensive knowledge are available here in abundance and that's what sets the market apart from other shopping outlets. Stall holders are passionate about their products and are keen to pass on knowledge and expertise to customers. It's an all-round experience that's hard to match and there's something available for everyone.

Sheffield's first Royal Charter to hold markets may have been granted in 1296 by Edward I, but the new premises and all it has to offer brings the Moor Market firmly into the 21st century.

Down on THE FARM

Some of us have a dream of living the idyllic country life. That's the world of pork genius Stephen Thompson and family – we're so jealous!

Povey Farm sprawls across 240 acres of prime farmland at the bottom of S8's winding Lightwood Lane.

Until 2007 it led a quiet existence run by Stephen and wife Karen, the fourth generation of the Thompson family to farm the land.

But deciding to present friends and family with home-grown ham that Christmas proved a fortuitous decision. Rave reviews, including cajoling from ex-Sheffield Star editor Alan Powell, encouraged the Thompsons to take the leap into producing fine meats for the market.

Karen enrolled on a butchery course and Moss Valley Fine Meats was born – with Stephen organising sales, deliveries and marketing. They initially sold to family and friends, but expansion quickly followed, and chief butcher of 30 years Mick was brought on board – enabling Karen to focus on caring for their pigs.

Moss Valley now supplies over 40 restaurants in and around the city. Butchering one pig every three weeks has grown to nine pigs every seven days. As well as bacon, joints, mince, ribs and more, this produces around a tonne of sausages – that's 7,000 a month.

Growth has sported numerous accolades, most recently Best Streaky and Back Bacon at Derbyshire's annual Bakewell Show, second place in the UK catering awards Sausage of the Year category for their breakfast banger, and Eat Sheffield's Brand of the Year.

Moss Valley
PORK THREE WAYS

This dish was prepared by one of our customers, chef Andy Gabbitas,
at The Wortley Arms. Serves 4

Ingredients

2 Moss Valley pork fillets

6 slices Parma ham

1kg pork belly

4 pork cheeks

1 Granny Smiths apple, cored and cut into 8

100g butter

30g brown sugar

Bag of spinach, wilted

For the bubble & squeak:

400g leftover mashed potato

200g leftover cooked mixed vegetables ie: carrot, cabbage, etc...

Method

Wrap the Parma ham around the pork fillets and pan fry until golden, then place in a medium hot oven at 180°c for 8 minutes, or until cooked through.

Place the belly pork on a trivet over an oven tray and roast in a hot oven at 190°c for 45 minutes, then turn the oven down to 170°c for 45 minutes and a final 45 minutes at 150°c – this will render away the fat and ensure a crisp skin. Cut into portion sizes.

Braise the pork cheeks in some beef stock at 160°c for 2 hours, or until tender. Strain and reduce the braising liquid to make a sauce.

Melt the butter in a frying pan until foaming, add the apples and colour until a golden brown, turn them over and do both sides and add the sugar to the pan, swirl to make a caramel then remove from heat.

For the bubble & squeak mix any leftover veg with mashed potato, shape into loose patties and pan fry until crisp and golden on both sides.

To assemble place the bubble and squeak on a plate, top with three slices of pork fillet.

Add one piece of belly pork, serve the braised cheek on a bed of wilted spinach add the caramelised apples and pour over some of the reduced braising stock.

Nonnas
KNOW BEST

They say Italians' do it with style. Add to that the determination and industrious nature of a Sheffielder and you get 'Nonnas'.

Sheffield's food scene reached a new high with the opening of Nonnas – an Ecclesall Road institution since 1996.

Acknowledged as the city's benchmark for great Italian food, the restaurant has built a solid reputation since it was opened by Gian Bohan and Maurizio Mori.

Authentic, great quality food, goes without saying. Traditional dishes, like lasagne and tiramisu, have been on the menu since day one, with a few tweaks and improvements along the way. These classics are complemented by a whole range of other dishes that incorporate creativity and technique.

The bar and restaurant is also noted for its wine list, which has been recognised in the AA and Good Food guides for a number of years, thanks to its support for indigenous grape varieties of Italy – which Gian believes are treasures to be uncovered.

But Nonnas is so much more than acclaimed food and wine. It's a whole entity that allows you to experience an authentic taste of Italy without setting foot outside Sheffield.

For those prepared to travel a little further, Casa di Nonnas – their guest house in the heart of Tuscany, Italy – offers a chance to be swept up in a gastronomic break combining trips to Gian's favourite restaurants or even to be accompanied by the man himself as your personal chef.

The restaurant's popular cycling team, La Squadra, is another integral part of the Nonnas community. The organically-formed club has its own club house and members meet regularly to cycle the neighbouring Peak District – even taking trips abroad together.

Combine each of Nonnas facets and it's not difficult to see why these ambassadors of Italy have stood the test of time.

Nonnas

established 1996

Pizza Slice
£2.95

Tagliatella SALSICCIA

Serves 4

Ingredients

500g Italian sausage meat

1 onion

1 clove garlic

¼ grated nutmeg

1 bay leaf

1 teaspoon dried chilli

400g passata

200ml cream

2 dessert spoons olive oil

375ml red cooking wine (we use Merlot)

480g fresh tagliatella pasta

Salt & pepper

Method

Dice the onion. In a pan, pour a dessert spoon of olive oil then add the onions, bay, chilli, nutmeg and garlic to brown.

Add the wine and reduce by half. Set aside.

In another pan, pour the rest of the olive oil, then brown the sausage meat. Once sealed, add to the wine and spices mixture.

Add this to your tomato passata, stir in well. Cook for around 10 minutes then add cream. Cook on a low heat for 8 hours, stirring occasionally.

Season with salt and pepper at the end. Set aside.

In a deep pan, boil water and add a little salt. Cook the pasta for approximately 7 minutes until just al dente, dress with the sauce then serve.

Nonnas TIRAMISU

Serves 6

Ingredients

For the base:

18 savoiardi biscuits

150ml strong espresso

5 tablespoons marsala

For the mascarpone cream:

3 large free range eggs, separate
eggs from yolks

5 tablespoons sugar

250g mascarpone

100ml whipping cream

Cocoa for dusting

Method

Place the egg yolks in a large bowl with the sugar and whisk until very pale.

Add the mascarpone and cream to the bowl and beat until thickened.

In a separate bowl, whisk two egg whites until peaks are formed.

Slowly add the whisked egg whites to the mascarpone cream, folding gently, mixing well but lightly. The cream should be soft and airy.

Now mix the marsala and the espresso. Dip each-side of the savoiardi biscuits one by one in the marsala/espresso, still keeping the savoiardi firm.

To assemble, layer the biscuits in a glass, then cream, then another biscuit until the glass is full and finish with a layer of cream.

Sprinkle cocoa powder on top to serve.

From dairy to DOORSTEP

We all know 'freshest is best' – and you can't get fresher than Our Cow Molly. Milk straight from the cow to your door on the same day.

History

Back in 2007, many dairy farms were struggling to make ends meet. The supermarkets' monopoly of buying power was forcing farmers to sell their milk at a price that only enabled them to break even at best.

Eddie Andrew, who'd recently moved back to his parents' farm at Dungworth, started looking for ways to diversify the business in order to combat the milk crisis. He visited The Dairy Show, a national trade event, and the answer presented itself to him in the form of ice cream.

He bought equipment from a family business which specialised in selling Italian ice cream equipment to farms. They even supplied a mentor: Italian ice cream chef Giuliano Hazan.

Alongside ice cream, the Andrews also deliver fresh milk to homes and businesses around Sheffield – getting their milk from cow to customer in a matter of hours. And so, Our Cow Molly was born.

Ice Cream Parlour

Our Cow Molly ice cream, stamped with the Made in Sheffield mark, can be found in over 50 outlets around the city – including Sheffield Theatres. But the Andrews' farm itself has become a favourite haunt for Steel City dwellers looking to indulge in their luxurious sweet treat. Visitors can even drop in on newborn calves and lambs while they're there.

A deluxe range of flavours is available, a number of which are only available at the farm parlour, including Wild Cherry Cheesecake, Bakewell Tart and The Sheffield Honey Company Ripple. A new special flavour is available each month. And the oddest flavour they've ever made? Brussels Sprouts! Created in support of an event for a charity cook book, 'Once a Sprout', the unusual flavour had people queuing up to try it.

The ice cream is made using roughly 19% cream and 53% milk – with the rest from concentrated fruit and other flavours. British-grown sugar, made from beet, makes up the rest of the product – meaning Molly's ice cream has a low carbon footprint.

GINGER BREAD
MAN

New Dairy

2014 will see the opening of Our Cow Molly's brand new dairy, which will increase production ten-fold and enable the farm to supply more Sheffield businesses.

And with the Andrews running the last remaining dairy farm in the city to bottle its own milk, support for them is imperative.

Milk bought through supermarkets can take around 5 days to reach a customer, by which time it is beginning to spoil and lose its nutritional goodness. But, as with their current dairy, the new facility will enable the Andrews to continue to supply what nobody else can – the freshest milk in the city.

Milking starts daily at 4am. The milk is immediately pasteurised and bottled, then town deliveries start from 9am. Buying milk from cows grazing the land helps to keep the countryside working and protect it.

Independent outlets already stocking Our Cow Molly milk have found it brings in repeat trade from customers who understand the benefit of buying super fresh milk, with many seeing their milk sales double.

National Open Farm Sunday

Our Cow Molly is open on various days throughout the week for visitors, but their involvement in the National Open Farm Sunday has become an annual attraction each June.

At every year's event, Our Cow Molly teams up with local businesses like Moss Valley Fine Meats and Bradfield Brewery and opens up the farm for a day of educational family fun.

Farm tours and tractor rides are available all day and you can even find Graham Andrew stuck in an animal pen for the Andrews' favourite 'Ask a Farmer' element of the day.

Visiting Molly, Lolly and the lambs goes without saying – as does indulging in the creamiest ice cream you've ever tasted, washed down with a glass of fresh, sweet milk.

Each year's date can be found on the National Farm Open Day website.

Our Cow Molly
BAKED ALASKA

All these ingredients can be sourced from independent shops and producers in Sheffield – make the effort, it's well worth it.

The name 'Our Cow Molly' came from a rhyme made up
by Eddie's father Graham:
"Don't put it in your supermarket trolley,
Buy your milk from Our Cow Molly."

Often asked by children if there is, in fact, a cow called Molly, the Andrews picked out their only pure white cow, with one black splodge. As if by fate, her calf turned out the same colour and has been affectionately named Lolly.

Ingredients

2 extra large Sheffield eggs

75g British caster sugar

50g British self-raising flour

225g British strawberries

1 litre Our Cow Molly ice cream, flavour of your choice

225g British caster sugar

Method

Pre-heat the oven to 190˚c.

Grease and line a 23cm sandwich cake tin.

Mix the eggs and 75g sugar in a large bowl until the mixture is pale in colour. Sift in the flour and then gently fold in. Transfer into the prepared tin and bake in the oven for 20-25 minutes.

Turn out and leave to cool on a wire rack.

Once cool, place the sponge on an ovenproof serving dish. Scatter with the strawberries, leaving a small gap around the edge. Slice the Our Cow Molly ice cream and arrange it in a dome shape over the strawberries. Put it into the freezer while making the meringue.

Pre-heat the oven to 230˚c.

Whisk the egg whites at full speed until they are stiff but not dry. Add the 225g sugar, a tablespoon at a time, still whisking at high speed until all the sugar has been added and the meringue is thick and glossy.

Take the cake and ice cream from the freezer and pile the meringue on top and over the sides, making sure that all the ice cream and sponge have been covered. Sprinkle over the flaked almonds. Bake immediately in the pre-heated oven for 3-4 minutes or until golden.

Dust with icing sugar and serve immediately.

The freshest & THE BEST

Peppercorn was always going to be a success.
Front of house Kelly providing the finesse and charm and head chef
Charlie turning out amazing dishes time and time again.

Peppercorn's head chef and co-owner Charlie Curran has over 25 years' experience.

After working his way up the chef food chain in establishments like Headingley cricket ground and Leeds' Hayley's Hotel, Charlie's big career break came in the form of a role in Brian Turner's London restaurant where he eventually became head chef.

Five years later Sheffield beckoned Charlie back, and he met partner and front-of-house expert Kelly Ware.

The couple moved on to a joint venture, running the Samuel Fox Country Inn at Bradwell, Derbyshire, where they earned two AA Rosettes and a Good Food Guide recommendation.

Aspiring to run their own restaurant, the couple realised their dream and bought Peppercorn on Abbeydale Road in 2013.

Everything is made in-house, including breads and chocolates, and produce is local, from meat and dairy to fruit and vegetables, ensuring freshness and quality in their menus – which change every couple of months.

Charlie's flair for creative dishes using seasonal and the best ingredients available and Kelly's expertise and easy rapport have already earned them an army of regulars who appreciate their unique blend of fine dining without stuffiness.

Belly pork with
SHEFFIELD BEST BITTER BLACK PUDDING

Ingredients

For the belly pork:

2kg belly pork (skinned and back fat removed)

2 pints of Sheffield bitter (we like Seven Hills from Sheffield Brewery)

2 medium onions

2 carrots

1 stick celery

3 sage leaves

For the black pudding:

1 pint double cream

250g dried pigs blood (ask your local butcher)

2g cinnamon powder

2g mixed spice

4g curry powder

80g plain flour

Method

For the belly pork:

Roughly chop one onion, carrots and celery. Place in a deep roasting tray with the sage. Place the belly pork on top.

Cover with 1 pint of beer and 1 pint of water. Cover in foil and roast in the oven at 110°c for 5 hours.

For the black pudding:

Dice the other onion as finely as possible then fry gently in a large saucepan with the cinnamon, mixed spice and curry powder until soft.

In a bowl mix the flour, dried pig's blood, the rest of the beer and the cream. Pour onto the onions in the pan and continue to cook slowly, stirring regularly as to avoid sticking. As it heats and thickens, it will become similar in texture to play-doh.

Remove from heat and place in a baking tray, lined with baking paper. Smooth until even and bake in the oven for 15 minutes. Remove and leave to cool.

When the pork is cooked, remove from the oven. Allow to cool for 1 hour or until safe to handle but not cold.

Carefully pull off strips of belly pork and place in a lined baking tray to create a layer. Cover with black pudding (one piece is best) then cover with remaining strips of belly pork.

Place another baking tray and weights on top to press the belly pork and black pudding together and chill in the fridge overnight.

Cut into desired shape and re-heat in a hot oven.

Serve with vegetables and potatoes of your choice.

Jane Fairclough's
RHUBARB BAKEWELL TART

Jane is a keen home baker whose daughter came to Sheffield to study – and, like many, ended up stopping here. As such, she makes regular trips to the city and has fallen in love with the local food scene – regularly dining out in Sheffield's independent restaurants and sourcing the best seasonal produce for her inventive recipes.

Jane won the competition in Exposed Magazine to have her recipe featured in the book – and a worthy winner she was at that!

Ingredients

500g rhubarb

75g caster sugar

Juice of 1 orange

For the pastry:

225g plain flour

125g cold butter cut into cubes

Pinch salt

2 egg yolks

½ teaspoon ground cinnamon

Ice cold water

For the frangipane:

110g butter

110g caster sugar

2 eggs

110g ground almonds

25g plain flour

½ teaspoon baking powder

Grated rind of 1 orange

Flaked almonds to decorate

Method

Pre-heat oven to 190°c.

Cut the rhubarb into 2cm lengths and toss in sugar and orange juice. Put on a baking tray and cook for 15-20 minutes, or until just tender. Drain and reserve the syrup then leave to cool.

To make the pastry, mix the flour, ground cinnamon and salt in a bowl, then rub in the cold butter until the mixture resembles breadcrumbs. Stir in the egg yolks and just as much cold water as you need to bring it together into a dough; it should not be sticky. Alternatively, use a food processor. Wrap in cling-film and chill for at least an hour.

Grease a 20cm loose bottom tin and roll out the pastry on a lightly floured surface until large enough to line the tin. Line pastry case with baking paper and weigh down with baking beans or dried pulses. Bake for 20 minutes then remove paper and beans. Brush with beaten egg and bake for a further 10 minutes until pastry is golden brown. When cold, trim off excess pastry to make a neat edge.

To make Frangipane put butter, sugar and orange rind in a bowl and beat until light and fluffy. Beat in eggs one at a time then fold in flour, baking powder and ground almonds.

Put cooled rhubarb in base of pastry case then spread the frangipane mixture over it. Arrange flaked almonds on top and bake for 30-40 minutes until golden brown and just set in the middle.

Serve warm with a little of the reserved rhubarb syrup and vanilla ice cream or clotted cream.

Sustenance
IN STYLE

Rowley's in Baslow, is a popular destination for discerning diners looking to indulge their tastebuds with some of Derbyshire's finest produce.

Discerning diners with a taste for classy food know to head to Rowley's at Baslow, Derbyshire, for superb cooking.

Rowley's is the relaxed, more rustic sibling of Michelin-starred Fischer's at Baslow Hall. Formerly the Prince of Wales pub, it was taken over by the Hall's proprietors, Max and Susan Fischer, and their executive head chef Rupert Rowley in 2006.

The pub, which has a picturesque setting on the edge of the Chatsworth Estate, was transformed into a stylish new bar and restaurant with contemporary décor and comfortable furnishings. The new gastro-pub quickly became a well-loved destination for diners in Baslow and the surrounding areas and has become a favourite place for a spontaneous lunch when visiting the Peak District.

Since its launch, Rowley's has built up an excellent reputation for simple cooking, well executed dishes, featuring fresh, wholesome, impeccably sourced ingredients: exactly the qualities on which Fischer's is founded.

It offers a range of special menus, including a set lunch, Wednesday Pie & Pint night and Friday fish supper. It also hosts a programme of special events and themed food nights.

The partners have worked closely with head chef Jason Kendra and sous chef Iain Woodhead to devise menus combining classics – including terrines and slow-cooked dishes – and some more innovative creations. All have a strong focus on quality that underlines the Fischer's philosophy.

Max himself can occasionally be found moonlighting at Rowley's and is an inspiration to the kitchen team. These days, he's also a keen gardener, and his love of seasonal produce has been integral to the restaurant's evolution – a fact that's been recognised by recent accolades which include being named Local Food Hero in the Derbyshire Food & Drink Awards and an honorary doctorate from Sheffield Hallam University.

"Pie & Pint" £12.75 EVERY WEDNESDAY! from 5.30pm

Braised oxtail with
CARAMELISED SHALLOTS AND
CARROT & SWEDE MASH

Serves 4

Ingredients

For the braised oxtail:

1 large oxtail, jointed

4 raw medium carrots, diced ½ cm

4 celery sticks, diced ½ cm

6 peppercorns

2 bay leaves

Sprig thyme

Small bunch parsley stalks

1 bottle red wine

1.5 litres beef stock

1 pre-cooked medium carrot, diced ½ cm

½ pre-cooked celeriac, diced ½ cm

½ pre-cooked swede, diced ½ cm

150g caul fat

For the caramelised shallots:

600g small shallots/baby onions peeled (leave root on top to hold onion together)

3 tablespoons olive oil

2 bay leaves

Sprig thyme

1 tablespoon maple syrup or honey

Chicken stock (enough to just cover the onions)

½ teaspoon chives, chopped

½ teaspoon parsley, chopped

For the carrot & swede mash:

250g carrots, diced to 1cm

250g swede, diced to 1cm

Salt & freshly ground black pepper to taste

75g butter

Method

Pre-heat the oven to 180°c.

Seal the oxtail in hot oil until golden brown. Remove it and add the raw diced carrots and celery. Cook until brown, then return the oxtail to the pan. Deglaze with red wine and beef stock.

Add the thyme, bay leaves, parsley stalks and peppercorns and cover tightly with tin foil or a lid. Place in the oven for 2 hours until the meat falls off the bone.

For the shallots, add all ingredients together in a pan and leave to simmer until stock has evaporated and the maple syrup or honey begins to caramelise the onion. Set aside until required.

To make the mash, put the carrots and swede in a saucepan with water. Bring to the boil, cover and simmer briskly for about 20 minutes until soft. Drain in a colander and pass through a fine sieve. Once you have the carrot and swede to your preferred texture add butter, salt and pepper and mix in gently. Just before serving, add ½ teaspoon each of freshly chopped chives and parsley.

Remove the meat from the cooking liquor. Pull the meat from the bones and pass the liquor through a fine sieve and reduce. Keep skimming all impurities off the top of the stock. Once reduced to a sauce consistency remove half and set aside. Keep reducing the remainder until it is a thick, sticky glaze.

Add the cooked vegetables and meat to the glaze. Roll into tennis ball size and wrap in caul fat, leave in fridge overnight to set.

To serve: Reheat the oxtail in the sauce in the oven until piping hot.

Reheat the mash and caramelised shallots.

The man of STEEL

Named after the founding father of one our most famous steel producers, The Samuel Fox Country Inn has a proud heritage. This is enhanced by talented chef James Duckett and his staff.

The Samuel Fox Country Inn is a hidden gem, tucked away in the quiet village of Bradwell, just half an hour out of Sheffield in the Peak District.

The inn is named after notable local, Samuel Fox Esq, who founded the Stocksbridge Steel Company and is credited with inventing the modern steel framed umbrella.

Now run by chef patron James Duckett, a respected chef with over 20 years' experience, the inn's food offering is what he describes as 'progressive country cooking'. Dishes feature punchy, robust flavours without the fuss of fine dining – a reflection of James' own tastes.

And these are tastes that have been honed by global experience. Born in Lancashire, James has since spent time in restaurants in France, Holland, Spain and Australia, all of which have influenced his cooking.

While local and seasonal go hand-in-hand for James, it's developing his food that inspires and challenges him. Many dishes return to his annual menu repertoire, but they're never the same – he persists in evolving elements time after time with a new twist.

Some of Sheffield's favourite local suppliers – Owen Taylor, The Herb Table, Bradfield Brewery – pop up on James' list, but he also forages fresh ingredients from the surrounding countryside: elderflower, wild garlic and wood sorrel all make their way on to the menus.

With four bedrooms available, the Samuel Fox has become a favourite destination for 'foodie walkers' from far and wide. But there's room at the inn for everyone, whether it's a good meal or just a simple pint you're after.

Roast cod fillet
ON A CASSEROLE OF CLAMS

Serves 4

Ingredients

600g Fresh cod fillet (skin on)

1 tablespoon rock salt

50ml Pomace oil

20g unsalted butter

1 lemon

800g clams

150ml dry white wine

50g carrot

50g celery

50g celeriac

50g fennel

50g onion

3 cloves garlic

Sprig thyme

Bunch chives

200ml double cream

Method

For the clams:

Soak the clams in cold salted water over night to clean and purge them.

The next day pour the clams into a colander and wash with cold fresh water. Check each clam is tightly closed. If any are open or broken then discard.

Soak the cleaned clams again in cold water and put in the fridge until required.

For the cod:

Remove any pin bones and sinew from the cod. Take a tray and lightly sprinkle rock salt on it.

Lay the cod fillet on top and sprinkle more salt on the flesh side.

Cover the fillet with cling film and refrigerate for one hour to remove excess moisture and firm up the flesh for cooking.

Remove from the fridge and wash gently under cold water then pat dry with a clean cloth.

Cut the cod fillet into neat 150g pieces, then place on a cloth on a plate until required.

For the casserole:

Peel the carrots, celery, celeriac, onions and dice into 1cm cubes.

Put a deep pan on a hot stove and add half of the pomace oil. Once hot, add all the vegetables, the whole garlic cloves and thyme.

Add a pinch of salt then the white wine.

Add the clams, cover tightly with a lid and steam until they open.

Once open remove the pan from the heat and pour the contents onto a deep tray to cool quickly. As they cool, start to remove the clam flesh from the shells.

Discard the shells and put the clam meat back in with the vegetables and wine.

Drain the liquid from the tray back into the pan and reduce to a quarter of its original volume.

When reduced, add the cream and simmer gently until it thickens to form a sauce.

Add the clams and vegetables back to the sauce after removing the garlic and thyme.

Meanwhile, chop the chives finely and cut the lemon in half ready for juicing.

Cooking the cod:

Pre-heat the oven to 180˚c.

Put a non-stick coated frying pan on a medium heat and let the pan reach full temperature.

Add the rest of the pomace oil to the pan and then place the cod fillet pieces skin-side down. There is no need to season the fish with salt but add pepper if you like.

When the flesh begins to cook and the skin starts to brown, place the pan in the oven for approximately 4 minutes until the fish is firm.

Add the unsalted butter and squeeze lemon juice on the fish. Baste with a spoon to glaze.

Finally, take the clam casserole and add the chives at the last minute so they retain their fresh taste and colour, then divide the casserole between four bowls and put the cod pieces on top, skin side up. Serve with some extra lemon and crusty bread.

Purely HONEY

On the moors. In your neighbours garden. Even at the city's museum.
The Sheffield Honey Company has hives all over our region,
bringing you the true taste of Sheffield.

The hum of honey bees fill the air and the heady scent of fresh honeycomb intoxicates the senses. A day in the office doesn't get more idyllic than this.

It's a daily experience for beekeeper and The Sheffield Honey Company founder Jez Daughtry. This luxury brand has become ubiquitous in and around the region since he launched it back in June 2010.

But the bee farming business wasn't always Jez's calling. He found himself drawn to the buzz of honey production after being made redundant from a successful IT career in 2009, and it was his childhood interest in beekeeping that led him to consider it as a full time occupation.

While IT might have seemed demanding, the 12-hour days, care of over 300 hives and the physical labour that The Sheffield Honey Company requires means Jez is working the hardest he has in his life. But it's all worth it for the finished product.

Jez now runs a successful artisan business producing blossom, soft set, heather and special edition honeys from hives located all over the city – look skywards and they can even be seen on the roof of Weston Park Museum. His empire also extends into the Peak District where they offer unique honey made from those hives in the national park.

For Jez, it's about making customers aware of honey and its provenance – the hard work put into it by him and his bees – is the priority: "I want people to see the genuine quality of our products and understand the difference between this and the honey you can buy in the supermarkets," he says. "I love the idea of everyone in Sheffield knowing where our honey comes from and having a jar in their cupboard."

And with Jez's busy bees making honey from flower nectar in our own back gardens, real local produce doesn't get much closer to home than this.

The Sheffield Honey Co.

WHITE CHOCOLATE, LIME & CORIANDER

Ingredients

For the white chocolate and lime mousse:

2 egg yolks

30g icing sugar

50ml lime juice

2 softened gelatine leaves

300g white chocolate, melted with a splash of cream

250ml cream

For the honey jelly:

The Sheffield Honey Company 100g blossom honey

100ml water

2 softened gelatine leaves

For the honey glass:

The Sheffield Honey Company 50g blossom honey

100ml water

For the lime and coriander gel:

100ml water

100ml lime juice and the zest of the limes

40g sugar

20g coriander leaves and their stalks

2g agar agar

Method

For the white chocolate and lime mousse:

Whisk the egg, sugar and lime juice over a pan of simmering water. When light and quite warm add the gelatine, fold in the warm chocolate and then the whipped cream. Place in moulds to set in the fridge.

For the honey jelly:

Heat the honey and water, add the gelatine and set in the fridge.

For the honey glass:

Heat together in a pan to 150°c, pour onto parchment paper and allow to cool. Blitz to a powder and sieve onto a baking sheet lined with parchment. Bake until melted then allow to cool a little before cutting and shaping.

For the lime and coriander gel:

Infuse the coriander stalks in the water and juice, add the sugar and dissolve.

Pass the liquid through a sieve, bring back to the boil, add the agar agar and mix thoroughly. Allow to cool a little then add the coriander leaves, put in a bowl and cool in the fridge.

When this has set, blitz until smooth in a blender.

Starstudded CAST

The Showroom, which opened in 1993, is the largest independent cinema in the UK outside London – and since prominent Sheffield chef Simon Ayres took over its kitchen in 2012 it's also earned a reputation for its food.

The simple, fresh food served up in the cafe-cum-restaurant is known for its creativity and flavours. Working with local suppliers and growing produce in the makeshift roof garden means that menus change with the seasons and everything, including the ice cream sold in the cinema, is made in-house – the only cinema in the country to do this.

Local suppliers include Cafeology, Whirlow Hall Farm, Moss Valley Fine Meats, Round Green Farm, Blue Bee and Abbeydale breweries.

The Showroom's cookery classes are testament to the popularity of its food offerings, with lessons in bread, pastry and chocolate regularly selling out.

This Steel City entertainment hub is a favourite local haunt in which to spend an entire evening, with great food, drink and entertainment under one roof.

Simon Ayres

Head chef Simon trained as a chef at Castle College. London beckoned after training and Simon explored his craft at restaurants and a country club in and around the British capital.

After being drawn back to Sheffield, Simon helped to open various restaurants and undertook freelance contract work.

Aside from revolutionising the Showroom kitchen he's best known for his 4 years at The Milestone – when he was one of the team which won the title of Gordon Ramsay's Best British Restaurant.

He has been at the Showroom since 2012 and is excited to continue developing the food and to show people that there's more to the cinema than meets the eye.

Jon Tite

Sous chef Jon has adopted Sheffield since he moved here in 2011. Having started out as a bar manager, he found himself pulled into the kitchen and realised this was his calling.

Jon has trained on the job and, as a lifelong vegetarian, has come to specialise in vegetarian food. He reached the final of the Vegetarian Society's Vegetarian Chef of the Year award in 2013.

Lisa Curran

Sheffield-born Lisa trained at Castle College to qualify in general catering. Her first job at Leeds' Hayley's Hotel & Restaurant ignited her love for pastry, which has been her speciality ever since.

Attracted by the call of the capital Lisa spent a year at Marasu's Chocolate Factory before becoming Gary Rhodes' second pastry chef and then Brian Turner's pastry chef.

She has over 20 years' experience and joined the Showroom in 2012.

FILM & FOOD

Leek and SAVOY CABBAGE BOUDIN

By Jon Tite – Sous Chef

Ingredients

150g crumbly cheese – Lancashire or Wensleydale

75g breadcrumbs

1 small leek, finely diced

1 small onion, finely diced

1 egg

1 egg yolk

1 teaspoon English mustard

3 teaspoons milk

1 small handful parsley, chives and oregano finely chopped

Salt & pepper to taste

4 Savoy cabbage leaves

Method

Add a splash of oil to a pan and over a low heat sweat off the leek and onion until the onions are translucent. Remove from heat and leave to cool until you can handle them.

Grate the cheese into a large bowl and add the breadcrumbs, mustard, herbs, seasoning and the leek and onion mix.

Lightly beat the eggs and milk and add to the dry mix.

Thoroughly combine all the ingredients using your hands and leave in the fridge for an hour.

Put a large pan of water on to boil. When boiling, blanch the cabbage leaves for 1 minute then remove and place in cold water to stop the cooking process. When cool remove and lay flat on a tea towel to remove excess moisture. Once dry, slice the leaves in half removing the thick central stem.

To shape the boudin:

Pull a 20cm length of cling film from a roll but leave it attached. Place the cabbage leaves across the cling film and overlapping by 2cm. Brush with egg yolk to seal. Spoon half the cheese mixture along the centre of the cabbage. Using the cling film roll the cabbage leaves over the mixture to form a sausage shape about an inch in diameter. Keep wrapping in cling film until you have a well wrapped sausage. Twist the ends of the cling film tightly to seal and the mixture has been pressed into a firm sausage. Wrap the whole thing in one last sheet of film to seal the tied ends up. Repeat until all mixture is shaped into sausages.

Turn the heat down on the water until it is gently simmering and add the sausages. They will take about 15 minutes to poach and will be floating when done. When cooked remove from the water and leave to cool and then refrigerate.

When ready to serve, slice the sausage into your required size and then pan fry in a little olive oil until golden.

Serving suggestions: with roast root vegetables and veggie gravy, with mash, as a replacement for the meat on a Sunday roast or simply in a buttie with wholegrain mustard.

Round Green venison liver
WITH SOUSED CHERRIES, PROSCIUTTO HAM AND RHUBARB

By Simon Ayres – Head Chef

Ingredients

For the liver:

600g sliced venison liver (Round Green Farm, Yorkshire Venison Centre)

2 cloves garlic

1 sprig thyme

1 sprig rosemary

Rapeseed oil for cooking

Salt & cracked black pepper to season

Sherry vinegar

50g butter

For the soused cherries:

100g fresh black cherries, pitted

200ml red wine vinegar

50ml Port

50ml Madeira

100g Demerara sugar

1 star anise

2 cloves

For the ham and sesame crisps:

4-6 slices prosciutto ham

1 teaspoon sesame seeds

For the confit rhubarb and dressing:

2 sticks rhubarb

2 tablespoons icing sugar

Orange peel

Method

For the liver:

Have ready thyme, garlic (peeled), rosemary, sherry vinegar, seasoning, rapeseed oil and a smoking hot pan. Season the liver with salt and pepper, sprinkle with rapeseed oil, place in a pan and cook on one side until dark and caramel in colour.

Turn after 1-2 minutes, add the garlic, thyme, rosemary cook for a further minute then add the sherry vinegar and butter. Keep basting the liver in the emulsified liquid. Take the liver out of the pan and rest before serving.

For the soused cherries:

These need preparing 24-48 hours before the meal to make sure they are fully infused.

Put all ingredients apart from the cherries into a heavy bottom pan and bring to the boil. Once boiled take off the heat and let the mixture cool.

Place the cherries into a kilner jar or jam jar, pour on the liquid, seal and leave in the fridge or a cool dry place to infuse for use later.

For the ham and sesame crisps:

Lay the ham on a baking tray lined with silicone paper. Sprinkle with sesame seeds, place another sheet on top and place another baking tray on top of that. Bake in the oven until crisp 150-160°c for about 20-30 minutes.

For the confit rhubarb and dressing:

Cut rhubarb to desired shape, saving the trimmings. Take a mixing bowl and roll the cuts of rhubarb in the icing sugar until completely coated. Add the orange peel and vacuum pack making sure the pieces are flat before vacuuming. Cook in a water bath at 65°c for 7 minutes until soft then place back in the fridge to chill for later use.

Iced honey cream
WITH DRIED FRUIT COMPOTE

By Lisa Curran – Pastry Chef

Ingredients

For the iced honey cream:

100g caster sugar

4 leaves gelatine

200ml double cream

The Sheffield Honey Company 200g Honey

25g cornflour

175ml water

10 egg yolks

7 egg whites

150ml orange juice

For the dried fruit compote:

75g dried apricots, soaked

50g dried prunes

75g dried figs

25g dried apple rings

1 cinnamon stick

4 star anise

6 whole cloves

The Sheffield Honey Company 100g Honey

200g granulated sugar

Peel of 1 orange

Method

For the iced honey cream:

Boil the sugar, honey and water, reduce until you get a thick syrup. Use while it's still warm.

Soak the gelatine in cold water.

Boil the cream, add the orange juice to the cornflour and mix well. Thicken the cream with this then add the yolks and cook for a few minutes.

Add the soaked gelatine, stir well, pass through a sieve and put to one side.

Make an Italian meringue by whisking up the whites with a mixer machine, then slowly pour on the honey syrup. Whisk until cold.

In stages, fold in the meringue to the custard mix.

Pour the mix into a tray lined with cling film then freeze over night.

For the dried fruit compote:

Put all the ingredients in a pan and cover with water one inch above the fruit. Boil until the fruit is tender and the liquid is syrupy.

Store in an air tight container in the fridge for up to 4 weeks. You can use from the fridge or use warm.

Place the fruit in a serving bowl, then add a piece of the iced honey cream.

You can eat it like this or finish under a hot grill. We use a blow torch to caramelise the top of the cream. Drizzle with honey.

The pride of YORKSHIRE

Silversmiths take local produce to a whole new level
– with all of their suppliers coming from 'God's own county'.

Self-proclaimed 'selectors of fine Yorkshire ingredients', provenance is Silversmiths' raison d'être.

For owner Justin Rowntree and head chef Lee Mangles there's nothing more important than sourcing locally – a blueprint given to them by mentor Gordon Ramsay following their participation in his Kitchen Nightmares series.

The team is proud to source meat, poultry and game from nearby farms like Round Green, Ewden, Whirlow Hall and Loose Birds Farm and locally caught game from Bradfield and Aston.

Lee even trudges out into the Peaks, kids in tow, for back-to-basics foraging for items like wild garlic, nettles, wild berries and cherries – which has now become a favourite family pastime.

Thanks to this dedication, 100% of their suppliers are Yorkshire-based, with 60% of those located in Sheffield – something they keenly pass on to customers old and new to inspire and encourage local sourcing, even for the home kitchen.

And, of course, hand-in-hand with local comes seasonal. The cyclic nature of Silversmiths' menus showcase the best of the best of local produce, from hearty beef pies to sumptuous rhubarb desserts, rich local cheeseboards and everything in between.

Lee and the kitchen team are also keen to give their guests the confidence to try new things for themselves, hence using unusual meat cuts such as their featured hogget dish, using a cut of two-year-old lamb.

Silversmiths' setting echoes the rustic nature of its offering, with stripped back reclaimed wood and atmospheric lighting from suspended storm lanterns providing a backdrop for plush ruby and ebony leather chairs.

This former cutlery works has been sympathetically refurbished to ooze character at every turn – from its heritage past to its current modern yet cosy incarnation.

And since its inception in 2009, the restaurant has added numerous accolades to its name, including runner-up for Best UK Restaurant in the Observer Food Monthly awards 2011, 2012 and 2013 plus consistent Good Food Guide entries.

Recognition hasn't come without that other key ingredient of a top class restaurant – good service. Hard work and genuine commitment have been put into building a 'family' of tight-knit staff with a low level of turnover, so customers old and new can always rely on seeing a face they recognise.

In fact the team spirit is so strong they even socialise together, sharing everything from the local pub quiz to holidays in Skegness, Amsterdam and Ibiza – taking their favourite local cabbie along for the ride.

Slow-braised lamb breast

MILK POACHED SWEETBREADS WILTED SAVOY CABBAGE & CARROT TEXTURES

We often serve this with Hogget, which is a farming term that refers to a sheep between the age of 1-2 years old. Serves 4

Ingredients

1 lamb (or hogget/mutton breast) (approximately 1.5kg)

100g sweetbreads (25g per person)

½ Savoy cabbage, finely shredded

12 Chantilly carrots (4 per plate), peeled & chopped

2 cloves garlic

100ml milk

Sprig rosemary

Sprig thyme

Method

For the breast:

Remove ribs from the breast (most butchers or farm shops will do this for you), trim off any excess fat, season and roll tightly into a sausage shape in cling film and tie each end. Place in a slow cooker or oven proof dish and cover with water, add a sprig of rosemary and garlic, cover and cook overnight (approximately 10-12 hours).

Remove from liquid, allow to cool, then re-roll and chill. Save the poaching liquid for later use.

For the sweetbreads:

Place them in a pan and cover with milk. Add the thyme, gently bring to the boil and simmer for 5 minutes. When cooked, plunge in cold water (this stops them overcooking). Once cooled peel off any fat or sinew.

For the carrot purée:

Place the peeled and chopped carrots in a pan then add enough poaching liquor to cover. Boil until tender. Place in a food processer and blitz until smooth, add butter and season to taste.

Add the carrots in a pan, cover with the poaching liquid from the lamb and cook until tender.

Put the thinly chopped cabbage into a pan with butter, salt and pepper then gently fry until soft.

To serve:

Portion the chilled breast into 4 equal pieces in an oven proof pan, fry each side to seal then add the carrots and sweetbreads, place the entire pan in a pre-heated medium hot oven for approximately 10 minutes, meanwhile heat the purée and cabbage (pan or microwave is fine). Place the purée on one side of the plate, place the breast on top, pile up cabbage next to the lamb, place the sweetbreads on top and carrots, serve with a rosemary or Henderson's gravy.

Chefs tip: Use the carrot peelings as a deep fried crispy garnish.

Yorkshire
RHUBARB FLAVOURS

Yorkshire is famous for the rhubarb triangle – an area between Wakefield, Morley and Rothwell known for producing some of the best rhubarb in the country. Serves 4

Ingredients

500g Yorkshire forced rhubarb

250g cream cheese

½ pint whipping cream

250g caster sugar

50g rice flour

1 egg

100g butter

175g self-raising flour

50g icing sugar

Method

For the rhubarb:

Trim off any excess leaves and cut the rhubarb into 2" batons. Place on a tray, sprinkle with the icing sugar and roast until tender. Remove 16 batons for garnish, and purée the remaining. Chill.

For the cheesecake:

Mix the cream cheese with 150g sugar, whip the cream and fold through the cheese, then ripple through three-quarters of the rhubarb purée. Place in a piping bag until needed.

For the "leather":

Pour the remaining purée onto a non-stick mat or greaseproof paper, spread thinly and place in a low oven, (75°c) dry in oven overnight, the longer in the oven the crisper the end product.

For the shortbread:

Cream the butter and sugar together until smooth, add the rice flour and self-raising flour to the mix, add the egg and mix well until all incorporated. Chill for around 30 minutes. Flour a surface and roll out thinly, cut out and bake for 12-15 minutes 160°c, place on cooling rack.

To assemble:

Place a piece of shortbread on a plate and pipe on cheesecake mix, repeat this process to form a tower (how tall is up to you). Garnish with the roast rhubarb and "leather".

Chefs tip: Any seasonal fruit can be used instead of rhubarb to recreate this dish.

Don't mess
WITH TEXAS

Inspired by adventures in the Lone Star State, Smoke Barbecue brings the taste of the deep south to the industrial heartland of Yorkshire – and does it in style.

Sean Gregory was so taken with the Texas barbecue restaurant he saw on TV that he took the next flight out to the US to check it out for himself.

With business partner Duka Nagy, he spent a week exploring the concept and the cooking – then flew back to Sheffield, determined to recreate it.

The result is Smoke Barbecue, their own take on the fire pit phenomenon; a taste of Texan hospitality in the heart of South Yorkshire.

Located beneath Sheffield's trendy 'cheese grater' car park in the city centre, the restaurant is unlike anything else in town. Diners are greeted by a sleek glass exterior and the enticing smell of oak smoke.

The lofty interior features tables constructed from old wooden pallets and barrels, walls lined with rusted corrugated iron, and lights made from washing machine drums. Diners are even encouraged to graffiti the toilet walls.

Centrepiece of the restaurant is the oak fire pit – set in Yorkshire stone – which creates an element of theatre.

The decor sets the tone for the rustic, wholesome food on the menu. All Smoke's meat is locally sourced, coffee comes from city-based Cafeology and ice cream from Yummy Yorkshire.

In true Texas style the focus is on meat. Joints are butchered, marinated and rubbed on site before cuts like ribs and brisket are smoked for 18 hours for melt-in-the-mouth perfection.

Approved by a passing Texan, who presented them with a dollar on their first day of opening, Smoke is Sheffield's authentic taste of America.

Smoke jalapeno
CORNBREAD MUFFIN

Makes 12 large muffins

Ingredients

600g plain flour

5 tablespoons baking powder

1½ tablespoons sea salt

700g polenta/cornmeal

240g caster sugar

700ml milk

240ml sunflower oil

3 eggs

500g sweetcorn, drained

1 cup jalapenos, diced

1 cup jalapenos rings for garnish

Maple syrup

Butter

Method

Pre-heat the oven to 180°c.

Sieve the polenta, flour, baking powder, sea salt and sugar together in a large bowl.

In a separate bowl beat together milk and eggs.

Stir the corn and diced jalapenos into the egg mix.

Gently pour the wet mix into the dry and leave to stand for 30 minutes.

Spoon the mixture into greased muffin tins to the top and put a couple of rings of jalapenos on each muffin to garnish.

Bake in a medium oven for 15-20 minutes – check in case they need longer as cooking instructions vary according to the oven used.

Serve warm with a small ramakin of maple syrup and one of whipped and piped butter.

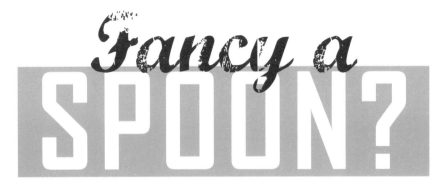

Fancy a SPOON?

If you wrote a wish list for your local café bistro, then what you would end up with is pretty much Spoon Bistro. Perfection on a plate.

Running restaurants is in the blood for Spoon's Jules Evans, who has over 25 years' experience working front of house.

Time spent honing his skills with restaurant chains, coupled with aspirations to own his own establishment, fuelled his fierce determination to build a restaurant focused on service, rather than financial gain.

And so in September 2011 Spoon was born. Jules initially spent six months alone in the kitchen turning his hobby of cooking into his profession.

His willingness to create anything a customer asks for, ingredients permitting, and the welcoming, homely atmosphere has increased Spoon's following. And to Jules' surprise it has organically turned into something he hadn't envisaged.

Daytime cafe-cum-evening bistro, there's something for everyone. The evening menu changes with the seasons and he tries to include dishes adaptable for people with allergies and dietary requirements.

Cakes, sauces, jams and soups are all made in-house and local producers' brands scatter the menu: from Our Cow Molly to Countryfresh, Batty's and Bradfield Brewery, money stays within the community where possible.

True to his word, customer interaction and satisfaction is paramount for Jules. He chats to diners as regularly as he can – and the appreciation shows. Just check out his growing museum of spoons and spoon-related artwork donated by customers the next time you're in.

Braised ham hock hash cake
WITH CREAMED LEEKS & SOFT POACHED EGG

Meaty ham hock with creamy mashed potato, topped with a soft poached egg –
this is our idea of heaven and one of our most popular dishes at Spoon Bistro.

Ingredients

1 ham hock roughly 1kg (we get ours from Batty's Butchers on Woodseats)

500g mashed potato (we use Maris Piper but any fluffy dry potato will work)

150g butter

2 leeks

2 level tablespoons of plain flour, buckwheat flour can be used to make this dish coeliac friendly

1 litre good chicken stock

Squirt of lemon juice (to personal taste)

6 free range eggs

1 spring onion for garnish

Method

To make the hash cakes: First wash the ham hock in cold water. Place in a large oven proof dish, covering the hock with cold water before putting on the lid. Place in a pre-heated oven at 160°c for 4 hours. When cooked, the meat should be falling off the bone and feel soft to the touch.

Leave to cool in the liquid for 30 minutes, drain through a colander discarding the liquid.

Peel and chop your potatoes, put in a large saucepan and rinse well under the cold tap. Cover the potatoes with cold water and add a pinch of salt. Bring to the boil then reduce heat to a simmer and cook for approximately 20 minutes until soft.

When cooked, mash the potato thoroughly with 75g of the butter (we use a potato ricer) until there are no lumps, then put to one side to cool.

The meat now needs to be pulled away from the bone discarding any skin. We tend to do this by hand as you will get more meat off. Combine the ham hock and mashed potato, about 60/40 meat to mash is our preferred ratio.

Cut the leeks down the middle then wash thoroughly. Chop into small pieces, roughly 2cm long, and combine a handful with the cooled hash mix. Form into 4-6 equal sized patties to make the hash cakes.

Heat some oil in a frying pan on a medium heat then fry the hash cakes individually for 2 minutes on each side or until golden brown. When cooked, place on a baking tray. Repeat the process until all of the hash cakes have been browned. Place in a pre-heated oven at 180°c for 15 minutes.

For the creamed leeks: Melt the rest of the butter in a medium sized saucepan and add the remaining leeks. Let them soften for 2 minutes, stirring so they don't burn, then add the flour and cook for 1 more minute to create a roux. Gradually add the chicken stock to the leeks until you have a sauce the consistency of double cream, check and season to taste.

For the poached eggs: Put a large pan of water on to boil with a dash of vinegar. Reduce to simmer and gently add your eggs to the pan one at a time and cook for 4 minutes.

To serve: Spoon equal amounts of the sauce on to plates then place your hash cakes in the centre, top with a soft poached egg, garnish with chopped spring onion and serve straight away.

Show me THE BEEF

The burger may be humble to some – but when it's been given the
Swanky Frank's treatment it's elevated to a gastronomic delight.

When Swanky Frank's opened its doors in Woodseats in
2010 it had one main aim – transform the humble burger
using fresh ingredients to create great taste combinations and
the best food around.

And Swanky Frank's' army of regulars would agree they've
achieved just that. Burgers are made using prime local beef
from John Crawshaw's, enveloped in air-light buns baked to
Swanky's secret recipe by a local artisan baker.

The menu also comprises other American favourites
including ribs, steaks and chicken as well as a dedicated
children's menu – plus – the obligatory American favourite
burger eating competition which has brought visitors from
the length and breadth of the country.

Swanky's also offer some regular creative events. One of
these is their 'Magic Mondays' – a unique evening of magical
entertainment where local magicians amaze you while you
make your meal disappear.

The restaurant, in a former coach house that's one of
Woodseats' oldest buildings, is the brainchild of chef Stuart
Berry, designer Paul Brady, restaurateur Marco Mori and
Stuart's brother-in-law Adrian Bagnoli, owner of city-centre
tapas bar Cubana.

Stuart, who's also Swanky's head chef, has led the kitchen
since opening. All the food is made in-house and specialities
include the delicious authentic Italian handmade pizzas by
their highly-skilled pizzaiolo Adriano Corso. All the food
can be adapted to individual tastes thanks to the kitchen's
flexibility.

This is a place where staff and customers know each other
by name and the atmosphere is always alive. Diners can be
assured of one of the warmest welcomes in Sheffield.

Swanky Frank's
BBQ & BURGER FEAST

The American diner experience is a great one and
Swanky's have shared their secrets with us.

Ingredients

For the BBQ ribs:

1 full rack pork ribs

2 tablespoons Cajun spice rub

1 onion, finely sliced

2 garlic cloves, finely sliced

2 tablespoons honey

2 tablespoons tomato purée

100ml BBQ sauce

100ml fresh orange juice

330ml Pepsi cola

For the Italiano burger:

8oz minced steak beef

1 teaspoon steak seasoning

Salt & pepper for seasoning

Top the burger with:

1 buffalo mozzarella, sliced

2 rashes Parma ham

1 seeded bun

Handful of chopped lettuce

1 tomato, sliced

1 red onion, sliced

Small handful of fresh basil leaves

For Swanky Frank's coleslaw:

1 small white cabbage, finely
shredded

3 onions, finely shredded

3 carrots, finely shredded

1 fennel bulb, finely shredded

3 tablespoons mayonnaise

1 lemon, juiced

Salt & pepper for seasoning

Method

For the BBQ ribs:

Coat the ribs in the Cajun spice rub and place under the grill to seal, turning once.

Remove and place into a large baking tray. Add the sliced onion and garlic along with the honey, tomato, BBQ sauce, fresh orange and Pepsi cola.

Cook in the oven for 3-4 hours on a medium gas heat, around 150°c.

For the Italiano burger:

Pre-heat the oven to 180°c and put the Parma ham in to crisp up.

Season the mince with the salt, pepper and steak seasoning. We use an 8oz portion per burger. Use your hands to make into burger shapes.

Grill the burgers until cooked through then top with the mozzarella cheese and Parma ham.

Serve in the seeded bun and garnish with lettuce, tomato and red onion. Finish with basil for a fresh taste.

For Swanky Frank's coleslaw:

Shred the white cabbage, onion, fennel and carrot in a bowl and mix in the mayonnaise, lemon juice, salt and pepper.

The Walkley GODFATHER

TV star, restaurateur, godfather... Vito Ciaraolo is an adopted Sheffielder with his roots in Southern Italy and his heart in Walkley.

Vito Ciaraolo first learned to cook as a boy in Bella, a town in Italy's Basilicata region. As an adult, he wanted to share a taste of his native culture and cuisine with the people of his adopted home in Sheffield.

The result was the opening of Vito's restaurant in 1991 – and Vito has been a popular part of the Walkley community ever since.

Known for his straight-talking, he believes his success has come from sticking to his authentic principles; serving food to diners the way it would be done back home.

Vito's cooking spans every region of Italy – recipes can vary greatly even from town to town – which makes for a great variety of flavours and techniques. Some of his favourite dishes represent his native southern Italy, but diners can also sample cuisine from Tuscany, Puglia and many other areas.

No expense is spared when it comes to ingredients. Venison fillet and lemon sole are regular features on the specials board, whilst meaty cod, king prawns and tender lamb all feature on the main menu.

Vito sources his ingredients and produce from other traders in Walkley, with his meat and bread coming from his neighbours.

The vast majority of diners at Vito's are regulars and have been visiting for over 2 decades. They are customers Vito

Vito Ciaraolo in costume for BBC drama Peaky Blinders.

has become very fond of: "I've seen young children grow up, marry and have their own families throughout their years of dining with me."

And, if Vito looks strangely familiar, that might be down to his TV debut in the gritty BBC drama Peaky Blinders – in which he played a sinister Italian gangster. He's Sheffield's very own Godfather of Italian cuisine.

Merluzzo Fiorentina
COD WITH ROASTED ALMONDS

Serves 2

Ingredients

200g fillet fresh cod per person

Olive oil

1 clove garlic

Salt & pepper

Splash of white wine

40g butter

½ pint milk

40g plain flour (or cornflour to make the recipe gluten free)

50g flaked almonds

Handful of spinach

Fresh basil

120ml cream

200g mozzarella

200g parmesan

Handful of coriander, chopped

Method

Pre-heat the oven to 200°c.

Melt the butter in a pan and add the flour a little at a time, stirring continuously to avoid lumps. Add the milk in small amounts and whisk to form a smooth white sauce and put to one side.

Heat olive oil in a pan until very hot, add a squashed whole clove of garlic and place the fish in the pan skin-side down. Season with salt and pepper to taste, then add a splash of white wine and cook until the skin starts to crisp. Turn the fish on each side for a couple of minutes and put to one side.

In the same pan, toast flaked almonds by adding a splash more oil and cooking over a medium heat for a couple of minutes until golden.

Make a sauce by combining the spinach, basil and cream and allow the greens to wilt.

In an ovenproof dish place a heaped tablespoon of white sauce per person and lay each fillet of fish on top. Sprinkle half of the almonds onto the fish then cover with the spinach and cream sauce.

Add a generous handful of mozzarella and parmesan to the top of the fish and bake in the oven for 10-15 minutes. The fish is ready when the cheese turns a golden colour or check by sticking a sharp knife through the fillet – it if goes straight through the fish is cooked.

Garnish the fish with the rest of the almonds and some chopped coriander.

At the heart
OF THE CITY

Georgian landmark the Wig & Pen has always been a popular drinking destination; but under the guidance of dynamic restaurateur Matt Bigland it's now fast becoming one of the city's best eateries as well.

Following the success of sister restaurant The Milestone in Kelham Island, owner Matt Bigland opened second venture the Wig and Pen in 2010.

Located in the heart of the city centre on Campo Lane, the Wig & Pen overlooks picturesque Georgian Paradise Square – the perfect backdrop at any time of year and particularly for the pub's popular summer barbecues. It's a sociable environment and an all-day venue frequented by couples and business people as well as families with children.

The stylish-yet-cosy interior allows drinkers and diners to relax and be looked after in comfortable surroundings while enjoying contemporary, seasonal food and one of the widest selections of wines and spirits in the city.

Sharing The Milestone's ethos, the Wig & Pen focuses on locally sourced produce to create its 'honest pub food' menu where everything is made on site.

The team is set to expand its love of local produce further still with the introduction of its 'garden to glass' cocktails – an innovative highlight to a new, seasonal drinks menu that will see herbs and garnishes growing on the bar ready to be freshly cut and used in their clever concoctions.

From breakfast to lunch, afternoon coffee to dinner, and evening drinks to celebrations in the Wig & Pen's private bar space, this city favourite offers something for everyone.

Pig terrine
WITH RHUBARB & CRISPY PIG SKIN

Ingredients

For the pig terrine:

4 ham hocks or 1 pig's head

1 large carrot, peeled

1 white onion, skinned and halved

2 sticks of celery

1 leek, halved

4 bay leaves

10 peppercorns

A few sprigs of thyme

250g caster sugar

Pommery mustard

Table salt

100g white flour

4 beaten eggs

250g Japanese breadcrumbs

For the crispy pork rinds:

1kg pig skin

25g Cayenne pepper

75g caster sugar

75g sea salt

50g smoked paprika

For the rhubarb jelly:

1 pint rhubarb juice

6 leaves gelatine

1 star anise

Caster sugar

For the rhubarb purée:

250g rhubarb, cut into small pieces

75g caster sugar

Lemon juice

Method

For the pig terrine:

Place the sugar in a heavy based pan and heat until you have a golden caramel. Add the vegetables and the ham hocks or pig's head and cover completely with cold water.

Add the peppercorns and herbs and slowly bring the pan to the boil, skimming any scum that rises to the top.

Simmer gently for around 2-3 hours or until the meat falls away from the bone. Leave it all in the pan together until it is cool enough to handle.

Remove any sinew, skin, bone and cartilage from the meat. Reserve the meat until needed and discard the rest.

Strain the cooking liquid through a fine sieve and return to the heat. Gently reduce the liquid by two thirds, again skimming any scum that appears on the surface.

Pass the liquid once again through a fine sieve then pour over just enough of it to bind the picked meat together (the natural gelatine in the liquid will help the terrine set.)

Add some mustard to the mixture to taste and season with salt if required. Mix well with your hands making sure there are no large chunks of meat left.

Line a roasting tray with a double layer of cling film, making sure there is a large overhang of excess cling film. Place the mixture in the lined tray and then fold over the excess cling film to cover it. Place another tray on top with a few kilograms of weight to press it firmly. Place in the fridge and leave to set over night.

Remove from the tray and cut in to desired shapes. Chill again until needed.

Place the flour, egg and breadcrumbs all in to separate bowls.

Roll the pieces of terrine firstly in to the flour, then the egg and finally the breadcrumbs making sure each piece is evenly coated. Reserve the coated terrine on a tray in the fridge until needed.

For the crispy pork rinds:

Place the pig skin in a deep pan of cold water, bring it to the boil and then simmer it until you can almost pierce your finger through the skin – this will take around 2 hours.

Remove the skin from the water and let it cool. Once cool scrape away all of the remaining fat from the skin. Place the skin on a cooling rack, then place in the oven at 60°c overnight until it is completely dried out. Reserve in an airtight container until needed.

Using a pestle and mortar blend all of the dry ingredients together.

Deep fry pieces of the dried skin until it has puffed up and is crispy, drain off any excess oil and season immediately with the dry seasoning mix. Keep in an airtight container until needed.

For the rhubarb jelly:

Gently heat the juice with the anise to infuse, meanwhile bloom the gelatine in cold water until soft. Season the warm juice infusion with caster sugar to taste, then stir in the soft gelatine. Pass the mixture through a fine sieve into a container lined with cling film and set in the fridge.

Remove the jelly and cut into desired shapes and sizes and keep refrigerated until needed.

For the rhubarb purée:

Toss the rhubarb in the sugar, place in a pan with a squeeze of lemon juice and cook over a low heat whilst stirring regularly until very soft. Place in a food processor and blend to a smooth purée. Pass through a fine sieve and chill until needed.

To serve:

Deep fry the pieces of bread crumbed terrine until golden and crispy. Season with sea salt.

Arrange some of the rhubarb purée, jelly, crispy terrine and crispy skin in a bowl. In the restaurant we garnish this dish with wild herbs and leaves, however you could garnish it with some salad leaves and edible flowers from your garden. This dish is a great light snack and is packed full of colour and flavour.

Feels like HOME

Masterchef of Great Britain Andy Gabbitas has built his solid reputation on great food served in a friendly environment with good local beers. What more does anyone need?

The Wortley Arms has been a cornerstone of this pretty village after which it was named for more than 250 years, but these days it's as well known for its food as it is for its history.

The Wortley family, of Norman origin, was in presidence of the grounds at Wortley and Wharncliffe Chase from as early as the 12th century. There's been an inn on the site since the early 1600s – but with the arrival of the turnpike road it was decided that a new hostelry was required.

Work started on rebuilding the Wortley Arms Inn on 11th May 1753 and was completed on 24th December at a cost of £188 6s 4½d.

The historical charm is retained to this day under Hillsborough-born chef owner Andy Gabbitas who's taken the inn to new heights since he took over in 2007. Cosy nooks and crannies and a sympathetic refurbishment gives the Wortley Arms a welcoming atmosphere, which is reinforced by its friendly family of staff.

Andy, a classically trained chef who has been cooking for nearly 40 years and has been a Master Chef of Great Britain for over 10 of them, brings a wealth of international experience to the table. Having worked as an army and private chef on yachts, his career has taken him as far afield as Hong Kong, Belize, New Zealand and Canada.

This is reflected in his seasonal menus, which combine both pub and restaurant food. Thai flavours are Andy's favourite and Asian-inspired dishes can be found alongside best-selling pork and venison. Local produce comes from Round Green and Meadow Farms, Moss Valley Fine Meat and John Crawshaw's butchers.

The Wortley Arms, which treats its customers like house guests, has gained and held two AA Rosettes since Andy took over. It's a fair bet that its place in both the village and food guides is guaranteed for a few years yet.

Round Green Farm
HAUNCH OF VENISON

The venison from Round Green Farm in Barnsley is amongst the best in the country and we have it on the menu as often as we can.

Ingredients

200g venison haunch

For the parsnip purée:

2 parsnips, peeled and diced

100ml double cream

100ml milk

For the wild mushrooms:

80g mixed wild mushrooms

50g butter

For the haggis bonbons:

1 haggis

100ml gravy

1 egg, whisked

Handful of breadcrumbs

For the potato dauphinoise:

1kg baking potatoes

4 cloves garlic

500ml double cream

Salt & pepper

Method

Boil the parsnips in the milk and cream until softened and then purée in a blender with enough of the cooking liquid to make smooth.

Sauté the wild mushrooms in the butter, season and serve.

For the haggis bonbons:

Cook your haggis as per manufacturer's instructions. Once cooled break up and mix with a little of the gravy to moisten and bind.

Mould into balls and pané in egg and breadcrumbs, then gently deep fry until golden brown.

Pan-fry the venison haunch in oil and butter until browned on all sides, season in the pan and then place in a hot oven for 3-5 minutes for rare. Remove and let rest for a further 5 minutes.

For the potato dauphinoise:

Slice the potatoes into thin slices. Finely mince the garlic and add to the potatoes with salt and pepper then mix well. Pour the cream over the potatoes and mix again.

Place the potato slices into a gratin dish, press down and bake for 1½ hours or until golden brown.

To serve:

Swipe some of the parsnip purée on a plate, place on a slice of the dauphinoise potatoes, cut the venison into five and place on the purée, place round some of the mushrooms, add a bonbon and drizzle over some of the gravy.

Easy like SUNDAE

Former chartered surveyor, Yee Kwan, takes her flavour inspirations from Chinese banquets and childhood trips to renowned Sheffield department store, Atkinsons.

The smoky tang of black sesame and exotic appeal of lychee ice cream may sound all Asian – but their maker is a Sheffield lass through and through.

Yee Kwan – a former chartered surveyor – creates her sweet treats by inspiration from childhood memories of Chinese family banquets… and trips to Atkinsons ice cream parlour in Sheffield city centre.

Honing her craft through demo days and master classes from gelato chefs, Yee is otherwise self-taught, dreaming up flavour combinations and recipes in her city-based production lab. Her 6.5% fat ice cream base is a revelation, meaning her desserts have only half the fat content of standard ice creams.

Yee Kwan's other unique selling point is undoubtedly distinctive Asian flavours. Green tea (using premium grade organic matcha powder) is the biggest seller, while Yee's Chinese customers can't get enough of her black sesame creation, which many say takes them back to their childhoods.

Yee Kwan's ice creams and sorbets are sold in over 200 restaurants and independent retailers around Sheffield and the UK – they're also stocked in Harvey Nichols, Wholefoods Market and Wing Yip Chinese Supermarkets.

As well as their own Happy Valley outlet in Sheffield's Moor Market, named after the Hong Kong district Yee's parents hail from, the ice cream can also be found in many local farmers markets and food festivals.

Yee Kwan – Sheffield lass she may be,
but chilling in the freezer requires plenty of layers.

Yee.Kwan

Honest Handcrafted Ice Cream & Sorbet

yeekwan.com

Yee Kwan Ice Cream

Yee.Kwan

Honest Handcrafted Ice Cream

BLACK SESAME SEED ICE CREAM

LYCHEE ICE CREAM

Macaroon
ICE CREAM SANDWICHES

Nothing is quite as scrumptious as eating an indulgent homemade macaroon ice cream sandwich. The fragrant aroma of the almonds and chewy texture of the macaroon works perfectly with our delicious artisan ice cream.

For an extra special sensory experience, you can add some fruity compote in the middle of the sandwich or roll the outside of the sandwich in some roasted chopped nuts, ground pistachio, almond brittle or ice cream sprinkles (available to purchase at our Happy Valley ice cream parlour in The Moor Market)

Ingredients

225g whole almonds or ground almonds

310g icing sugar

6-7 large free range egg whites

¼ teaspoon fine sea salt

125g granulated sugar

a few drops of food colouring (optional)

500ml tub of your favourite Yee Kwan ice cream

Fruity compote (optional)

300g your choice of fruit (raspberry, blueberries, peaches, strawberries)

3 tablespoons sugar

Squeeze lemon juice

Method

For the macaroons:

Line a large baking sheet with parchment paper. Using a 3" biscuit cutter as a guide, trace 12 circles on the parchment. (you want all the macaroons to be the same size, so you have perfect sandwiches). Turn the sheet of parchment over.

For people with plenty of time and a food processor.

Grind the nuts with 30g of the icing sugar in a food processor until you have a fine nut flour, do not let the mixture become a paste.

Add the remaining 280g of icing sugar and pulse until incorporated. If necessary, strain the mixture through a sieve.

For people that are in a hurry just substitute the whole almonds for ground almonds.

Mix the ground almonds with 310g icing sugar

Whip the egg whites and salt in a large bowl until frothy. Keep mixing and slowly add the granulated sugar, about one tablespoon at a time and whip the meringue until shiny and holds medium peaks.

Using a rubber spatula, fold in the almond mixture one third at a time until thoroughly combined. Be as adventurous as you like by adding a few drops of food colouring.

You will need a piping bag with a ¼ inch plain tip. Carefully fill the bag with the batter until half full. Hold the bag upright and start piping a spiral in the traced circles, starting from the centre of the circle and work your way out.

Pre-heat the oven to 150˚c.

Let the macaroons sit at room temperature for 30 minutes, this will create a lovely crisp crust on the outside of the macaroon.

Bake the macaroons for 18-20 minutes, rotating the tray halfway through. They should have risen slightly and look crisp and set on top.

Remove from the oven and let them cool completely.

To freeze the macaroons, carefully slide the macaroons from the parchment and pop them in a freezer bag or airtight container. They are very delicate so handle carefully.

To assemble the sandwiches:

Pop the frozen macaroons upside down, place a small scoop of ice cream on each of the cookies and top with another macaroons. Gently press them together and pop them in an airtight container in the freezer until ready to eat.

James Hargreaves'
ALL DAY BAKED BREAKFAST

James is an alumni of Sheffield Hallam University. A digital media professional who has held key roles with My Job Group and Sheffield Wednesday FC. he's been involved in several well known city web projects including Owlstalk, Sheffield History and Sheffield Band.
He describes his dish as "... the nicest breakfast you will ever, EVER have ... guests will think you are a culinary god, yet it is so easy to make!" Serves 2

Ingredients

2 slices of bread

8 rashes Moss Valley smoked bacon

2 Moss Valley sausages

2 large eggs

Handful of your favourite grated cheese (I used a strong cheddar)

Splash Henderson's Relish

Twist freshly ground black pepper

Method

Pre-heat the oven to 190°c.

Use a little spray oil to coat the edges and bottom of couple of individual pie dishes. Pop the sausages and bacon into a frying pan to colour Don't cook through, as they'll be going in the oven.

Remove the crusts from the bread shape into the bottom of the pie. Don't squash down too much, leave a little give in the bread.

Take the sausage and bacon and drain on paper towels. Line the edges of the pie dish with the bacon to form a border.

Grate a little cheese on top of the bread and add a splash of Henderson's Relish and a twist of pepper.

Dice the sausage into 3-4cm chunks and place in the dish on top of the cheese. If you've any bacon left you can pop some in the middle around the sausages too. Leave a little space on top for the egg.

Crack the eggs and pour into the top to fill the rest of the space (try to leave the yolk intact if you can, for runny egg!). Leave a little bacon and sausage sticking out the top for presentation and also to add a bit of crispy crunch texture to the dish when eating.

Sprinkle a little more of the cheese on top, and add a bit more Henderson's Relish and black pepper.

Place in a hot oven for 20-25 minutes or until the egg white sets but the yolk is still runny.

Serve on a layer of baked beans and run a little brown sauce over the top.

If you want to be even fancier, do the same in muffin tins (reducing the ingredients in each one, obviously) and serve as breakfast-style canipes.

The DIRECTORY

These great businesses have supported the making of this book; please use them where possible.

Ashoka
307, Ecclesall Road, Sheffield, S11 8NX
Telephone: 0114 268 3029
Website: www.ashoka1967.com
One of the oldest Indian restaurants in Sheffield, a true classic.

Baldwin's Omega
Brincliffe Hill, Sheffield S11 9DF
Telephone: 0114 255 1818
Website: www.baldwinsomega.com
The north's greatest banqueting venue run by the legendary 'Big Un'.

Beeches of Walkley
290 South Road, Sheffield S6 3TE
Telephone: 0114 234 0066
Website: www.wedoliver.com
High class, locally sourced products with free delivery in and around Sheffield.

Bloo 88
182 West Street, Sheffield S1 4ET
Telephone: 0114 270 6264
Website: www.bloo88.com
Stunningly renovated bar serving up the finest pizzas, cocktails, private parties and good times right in the heart of the city centre.

Cafeology
Unit 8, Woodseats Close,
Sheffield S8 0TB
Telephone: 0114 255 8007
Website: www.cafeology.com
100% ethical coffee that tastes great too.

Casa Hotel
Lockoford Lane, Chesterfield S41 7JB
Telephone: 01246 245 999
Website: www.casahotels.co.uk
Chesterfield's only 4 star hotel serving produce straight from their own farm.

Cubana
34 Trippet Lane, Sheffield S1 4EL
Telephone: 0114 276 0475
Website: www.cubanatapasbar.co.uk
Authentic Cuban ambience mixed with delicious tapas.

Cutlers Spice
1 Leighton Road, Sheffield S14 1SP
Telephone: 0114 241 6641
Website: www.cutlersspice.co.uk
A modern and luxurious Asian restaurant, either eat in or takeaway.

Eat Sheffield
Sheffield Hallam University,
Stoddard Building, City Campus,
Howard Street, Sheffield, S1 1WB
Telephone: 0114 225 3370
Website: www.eatsheffield.com
Committed to supporting the local and independent food and drink industry, including restaurants, manufacturers, producers and retailers.

Fancie
359-361 Ecclesall Road,
Sheffield S11 8PF
Telephone: 0114 266 3311
Website: www.fancie.co.uk
A stylish and homely atmospheric restaurant on the vibrant Ecclesall Road.

Fischer's at Baslow Hall
Calver Road, Baslow DE45 1RR
Telephone: 01246 583259
Website:www.fischers-baslowhall.co.uk
Michelin-starred for a reason. Stylishly tranquil, fabulously friendly and something a little different.

The Florentine
Tapton Park Road, Sheffield S10 3FG
Telephone: 0114 230 8692
Website: www.theflorentinepub.com
A striking building in stunning surroundings producing great food.